TABLE OF CONTENTS

★ ★

★ ★

President Barack Obama
The White House
1600 Pennsylvania Avenue, NW
Washington, DC 20500

Dear Mr. President:

It is a great honor and privilege to submit to you the report of the White House Council for Community Solutions (the Council), *Community Solutions for Opportunity Youth*. When you created the Council by Executive Order in December 2010, you asked the Council to help identify and raise awareness of effective community-led solutions to our nation's most serious problems. The Council engaged in intensive fact-finding and listening efforts and ultimately chose to address an area of critical importance to America's future: putting every young person on a clear path to economic opportunity.

During today's challenging economic times, too many families and communities across the country are struggling to make ends meet and to simply do more with less. In fact, the unemployment rates for young Americans—who are typically less skilled and new to the workforce—are at historic highs. However, your administration's commitment to creating jobs for Americans is moving the needle and helping create new opportunities for all Americans to get back on track. The Council's work complements other administration efforts by focusing on creating opportunity where it is needed most: in support of opportunity youth.

The Council concluded that it could draw attention to the promise of these young people and the actions that can tap their potential to contribute to our economy and society. The Council sees these young people—the 6.7 million 16 to 24 year olds (roughly one in six in this age group)—who are disconnected from both school and jobs as opportunity youth. Through our outreach efforts, we heard directly from and were struck by the tremendous response from citizens, cities, and community and corporate partners around the nation who stand ready to take action and do something to help make a difference in the lives of these young people.

Opportunity youth are isolated from the paths that can lead to economic independence. Moreover, the cost to the nation of inaction is high. According to a study commissioned by the Council, when lost revenue and direct costs for social supports are factored in, taxpayers will shoulder roughly $1.6 trillion over the lifetimes of these young people. Absent action, their futures are at risk—and collectively our nation's future prosperity is put at risk.

The report presents recommendations for successful community-led solutions across the nation: driving development of more successful community collaboratives to harness the potential of these young people; creating shared national responsibility and accountability; engaging youth as leaders in the solution; and creating more robust on-ramps to employment. We know that with training and support, opportunity youth hold enormous promise to infuse our economy with new skills and leadership, and they are eager to accept responsibility for their lives. The Council believes that the actions identified in this report, coupled with a nationwide awareness of the issue, will lead to significant progress toward putting all of our young people on a path to prosperity. At a minimum, we believe implementing the Council's recommendations will lower the number of opportunity youth by 10 percent.

On behalf of the members of the White House Council for Community Solutions, we thank you for this opportunity to identify and address a matter of critical importance to the nation.

Patricia Stonesifer
Chair
White House Council for Community Solutions

White House Council for Community Solutions
1201 New York Ave., NW
Washington, DC 20525

Dear White House Council Members:

Thank you for inviting us to review this report and contribute to its innovative recommendations for actions to improve the lives of the nation's opportunity youth.

As young people who have faced challenges in our lives, we don't often have the opportunity to be heard. When we first became part of the National Youth Ambassadors program organized by the Youth Leadership Institute (YLI), we were not sure that our opinions would matter.

As we contributed to the Council's work and developed our skills as spokespeople and leaders, we discovered that our voices do in fact matter a great deal. The highlight was having the opportunity to provide input on the draft of the final report recommendations and to see our ideas incorporated in the final report.

This note is our way of expressing our appreciation for the chance to have our say. We now know that our opinions, experiences, and stories do matter, and that our ideas, solutions, and work in our community will make a difference.

The three of us who attended the Summer Jobs+ Summit earlier in the year were moved by the experience. At that event, and in the months since, all Youth Ambassadors have become part of the national conversation on how to help opportunity youth get connected to education and employment pathways that ensure success and allow us to contribute to our families and our communities. As highlighted in the report, young people can and want to be part of designing community solutions to the challenges we face.

In closing, we want to say that we know the work does not stop here. We look forward to inspiring other youth to be problem solvers in their communities, and to ensuring that there is "no decision about us, without us."

Sincerely,

The YLI Youth Ambassadors

Jairus Cater, Nashville, Tennessee
Ryan Dalton, New Orleans, Louisiana
Trevor Easley, Columbus, Ohio
Francisco Garcia, Hacienda Heights, California
Torres Hughes, Chicago, Illinois
Shaakirah Medford, New York, New York

Jose-Luis Mejia, San Francisco, California
Brian Nguyen, Seattle, Washington
Hannah Sharp, Indianapolis, Indiana
Brittany Woods, La Mirada, California
Hashim Yonis, Minneapolis, Minnesota

LIST OF COUNCIL MEMBERS

★★

First Lady Michelle Obama, Honorary Chair, White House Council for Community Solutions

Patricia Stonesifer, Chair, White House Council for Community Solutions, philanthropic advisor

Byron Auguste, Director, Social Sector Office, McKinsey & Company

Diana Aviv, President and CEO, Independent Sector

Paula Boggs, retired executive, Starbucks; philanthropist; musician

Jon Bon Jovi, musician, Bon Jovi; Board Chair, Jon Bon Jovi Soul Foundation

John Bridgeland, President and CEO, Civic Enterprises

James Canales, President and CEO, James Irvine Foundation

Scott Cowen, President, Tulane University

John Donahoe, President and CEO, eBay Inc.

Michael Fleming, Executive Director, David Bohnett Foundation

David Friedman, Director and Chair, Edison Properties/HNB Private Trust

Jim Gibbons, President and CEO, Goodwill Industries International, Inc.

Michele Jolin, Senior Fellow, Center for American Progress

Michael Kempner, Founder, President and CEO, MWW Group

Steven Lerner, Founder and Managing Partner, Blue Hill Group

Maurice Miller, Founder and CEO, Family Independence Initiative

Laurene Powell Jobs, Co-Founder and Board President, College Track

Norman Rice, CEO, Seattle Foundation

Kristin Richmond, Founder and CEO, Revolution Foods

Judith Rodin, President, Rockefeller Foundation

Nancy H. Rubin, Board Member, National Democratic Institute

Paul Schmitz, CEO, Public Allies

Jill Schumann, Principal, ParenteBeard LLC

Bobbi Silten, Senior Vice President, Global Responsibility Gap Inc.; President, Gap Foundation

Bill Strickland, Founder and CEO, Manchester Craftsmen's Guild

Laysha Ward, President, Community Relations and Target Foundation; Board Chair, Corporation for National and Community Service

★★

INTRODUCTION

★★

Across the nation, individuals and community groups are working together to find new and effective solutions to local problems. Recognizing that the best ideas do not come from Washington but from communities, President Obama created the White House Council for Community Solutions in December 2010 by Executive Order to encourage the growth and maximize the impact of innovative community solutions and civic participation.

The White House Council for Community Solutions (the Council) was charged with: identifying key attributes of successful community solutions; highlighting best practices, tools, and models of cross-sector collaboration and civic participation; and making recommendations on how to engage all stakeholders in community solutions that have a significant impact on solving our nation's most serious problems.

Executive Order 13560 also directed this diverse group of leaders from various sectors to identify specific policy areas in which the federal government is investing significant resources that lend themselves to cross-sector collaboration. The Council, therefore, focused its attention on the broad question of what drives successful community solutions: those making greater than 10 percent progress on a metric. Next it focused on applying these findings to create substantial opportunity for disconnected youth. The Council chose this often overlooked population because of the untapped potential of these young people and the high cost to our nation. The 6.7 million disconnected youth[1] cost our nation approximately $93 billion in direct and indirect social costs in 2011 alone, making this issue both compelling and urgent. While all youth have potential, connecting these youth to education or employment will change the trajectory of their lives, as well as benefit their community and our nation as a whole.

In its outreach and listening sessions, the Council discovered these young people have energy and aspirations and do not view themselves as disconnected. To the contrary, they are eager to participate in their communities, in fact, to own the development of their lives. They want to create a successful future but need the tools and opportunities to create that success. To acknowledge their untapped potential, the Council chose to refer to this population as opportunity youth.

---

1 The literature, including reports for the U.S. Congress, characterizes young people 16 to 24 years old who are out of school and work as disconnected youth.

★★

The Council approached its work in three phases:

Phase One: Fact-finding and listening efforts to establish knowledge base. *(December 2010-June 2011)*

The Council reviewed data-driven research and conducted extensive outreach to understand successful community-based groups of organizations working together (community collaboratives) and the demographics, needs, and existing programs for opportunity youth. The most compelling input came from young people themselves, but the Council also spoke with more than 300 organizations, families, mentors, businesses, social sector organizations, and government agencies that serve youth. The Council also conducted site visits to community collaborations that are achieving significant progress on persistent community issues.

Phase Two: Leveraging knowledge base to develop and launch resources. *(June 2011–January 2012)*

In fulfilling elements of the Executive Order, the Council identified gaps in information and resources to support community solutions. As a result, the Council developed the following resources to build awareness and assist communities. (All resources are available at http://www.serve.gov/council_resources.asp#maincontent.)

- *Community Collaboratives Toolbox.* Includes best practices, tools, and models for effective collaborative approaches.

- *Employer Tool Kit: Connecting Youth to Employment.* A simple guide for employers to create a mutually beneficial youth engagement program.

- *The Economic Value of Opportunity Youth.* A report on the size of the population of opportunity youth, the cost of inaction to taxpayers and society, and the benefits of reinvesting in these young people.

Phase Three: Building awareness, shining the spotlight on what works, advocating for greater systemic change to support success, and listening to feedback. This knowledge was used to develop the Council's recommendations to the President. *(January 2012–June 2012)*

The Council worked across sectors to build awareness of the data, tools, and the path forward through personally leveraging a wide variety of media opportunities, participating in Opportunity Community Conversations hosted by more than 30 United Way local affiliates, and participating in a White House Youth Summit to bring youth, key leaders, and change-makers together to commit to action.

Through its work, the Council has fulfilled its mandate and presents in this report its key findings and resulting recommendations to drive the creation of more successful collaboratives in communities across the nation. This report also provides an assessment of opportunity youth in our nation, as well as four core strategies – driving the development of successful cross-sector community collaborations, creating shared national responsibility and accountability, engaging youth as leaders in the solution, and building more robust on-ramps to employment – with accompanying recommendations for reconnecting these youth to successful careers and civic lives that will benefit themselves as well as their communities and our nation as a whole.

EFFECTIVE COMMUNITY SOLUTIONS

——— ★ ★ ———

Consistent with the administration's view that the most innovative, effective solutions come not from the federal government but from communities themselves, the Executive Order directed the Council to identify key attributes of effective community-developed solutions to our national problems.

Recognizing that despite good intentions and examples of success, most community efforts fail to achieve significant results, the White House Council for Community Solutions worked with The Bridgespan Group to identify collaboratives that have actually moved the needle, or created more than a 10 percent improvement on a community-wide metric, to understand what makes them effective, and to determine whether these key characteristics could be adopted by other communities seeking greater impact. The analysis identified a dozen communities across the country where all sectors have pulled together to make more than 10 percent progress on a community-wide metric, and more than 100 additional communities that are making progress in this direction.

> We have to recognize
> that to transform
> young people's lives,
> it's not individual programs
> or individual interventions;
> it's communities and
> supportive relationships.
>
> *– Paul Schmitz*
> *CEO, Public Allies*

Individual nonprofit services can be fragmented and dispersed, with each organization typically serving a limited population with specific interventions. Funders then measure success at the organizational level, rather than the broader community level. These individual efforts are critical to the lives and well-being of the people they serve and are important examples of success to demonstrate that progress is possible. But overall, these approaches are not resulting in significant change at a community-wide level, which is frustrating to all: taxpayers, funders, policy makers, service providers, and the beneficiaries themselves.

America has a long history of community revitalization efforts that were groundbreaking and changed the lives of many individuals, helping shape the work of successful efforts today. Communities can point to numerous examples of collaborations created to solve local problems. But only recently have we begun to see needle-moving collaboratives that are data-driven and highly focused on aligning existing resources toward a common set of targets for community-wide change.

To better understand these collaboratives, The Bridgespan Group and Council members conducted extensive research to understand this work and inform its recommendations, including a review of more than 100 high-potential collaboratives, site visits to a number of community collaboratives that have achieved significant needle-moving change, interviews, and a day-long meeting with leaders of community collaboratives and national organizations that support their work.

——— ★ ★ ———

To ensure evidence-based results, each profiled collaborative underwent a structured due diligence process. This involved external research and exploratory conversations with the collaborative followed by site visits or in-depth discussions. While the Council sought to be inclusive in its search, the resulting list of proof points is not exhaustive.

Through this research, the Council developed a Community Collaborative Framework (see Exhibit 1) that serves as a road map for success for other communities across the country to effect large-scale change.

Based on these findings, the Council believes that community collaboratives with these identified attributes should be replicated to address complex, persistent social issues in communities across the nation.

Exhibit 1: Effective Community Solutions

CORE PRINCIPLES	CHARACTERISTICS OF SUCCESS	SUPPORTIVE RESOURCES
What type of collaborative are we talking about?	**What do successful collaboratives have in common?**	**What do they need to thrive?**
Collaboratives with: • Aspiration to needle-moving (e.g., 10 percent +) change on a community-wide metric • Long-term investment in success • Cross-sector engagement • Use of data to set the agenda and improve over time • Community members as partners and producers of impact	• Shared vision and agenda • Effective leadership and governance • Deliberate alignment of resources, programs and advocacy toward what works • Dedicated capacity and appropriate structure • Sufficient resources	• Knowledge • Tools • Technical assistance from peers/experts • Policy • Funding

CORE PRINCIPLES OF NEEDLE-MOVING COLLABORATIVES

In addition to sharing a commitment to needle-moving change, these collaboratives had the following operating principles in common:

- Commitment to long-term involvement. Successful collaboratives make multi-year commitments because long-term change takes time. Even after meeting goals, a collaborative must work to sustain them.

- Involvement of key stakeholders across sectors. All relevant partners play a role, including decision-makers from government, philanthropy, business, and nonprofits, as well as individuals and families. Funders need to be at the table from the beginning to help develop the goals and vision and, over time, align their funding with the collaborative's strategies.

- Use of shared data to set the agenda and improve over time. Data are central to collaborative work and are the guiding elements for collaborative decision-making.

- Engagement of community members as substantive partners. Community members are involved throughout the process in shaping services, offering perspectives, and providing services to each other, not just as focus group participants.

Community Collaborative Success: Increasing High School Graduation and College Enrollment Rates

The Strive Partnership, a cross-sector collaboration focused on "cradle-to-career" education, has achieved an increase of 10 percent on high school graduation rates and 16 percent on college enrollment since 2006. Cincinnati's students were falling behind in college readiness, with Ohio ranked 42nd in the nation for bachelor's degrees. The president of the University of Cincinnati joined KnowledgeWorks, a community foundation, and the local United Way to understand the problem and plot a path forward. They created Strive, made up of multiple collaborative networks, linked to an overall student road map of success, and outlined research-based milestones for kids from cradle to career. A shared vision, deep research, and data-driven planning and evaluation were several important factors that made the program succeed. Strategically aligning existing resources against cradle-to-career needs has led to 40 of the 54 identified indicators moving in a positive direction with several including college enrollment rates increasing by more than 10 percent.

White House Council for Community Solutions. *Case Studies of Effective Collaboratives*. 2011. http://www.serve.gov/new-images/council/pdf/comm_collabs_case_studies.pdf

---

CHARACTERISTICS OF SUCCESS OF NEEDLE-MOVING COLLABORATIVES

After conducting deeper research into the 12 needle-moving collaboratives, five common elements emerged as essential to their success. (See Exhibit 1)

- Shared vision and agenda: finding the common denominator. Developing a common vision and agenda are two of the most time-consuming and challenging of all the tasks a community collaborative undertakes. They are also two of the most vital. Establishing quantifiable goals can catalyze support and build momentum, and developing a clear road map can help organizations look beyond narrow institutional interests to achieve community-wide goals.

- Effective leadership and governance: keeping decision makers at the table. Successful collaboratives need a strong leader to fully engage stakeholders and coordinate their efforts. The biggest challenge is not so much bringing decision makers to the table, but keeping them there for years of hard work ahead. To achieve such a feat, it is important for the collaborative's leader to be respected highly by the community and viewed as a neutral, honest broker. In addition, the leader must work to create and maintain a diverse, inclusive table where both large organizations and small grassroots organizations have powerful voices.

> ## Community Collaborative Success: Reducing Teen Pregnancy
>
> **Teen Pregnancy Prevention Oversight Committee**, a nonprofit-led collaborative, resulted in a 31 percent drop in the teen birthrate over five years. In 2006, Milwaukee had one of the highest birth rates among teens in the United States. Convened and staffed by the United Way of Greater Milwaukee, the collaborative was co-chaired by the editor of the local Milwaukee paper and the health commissioner. Together, they set an ambitious goal to reduce the rate by 46 percent by 2015. Leadership and governance were critical elements: as a trusted and neutral party organization with its own staff and funds, the local United Way was positioned uniquely to convene the group. The 31 percent drop in the birth rate to date is significant as national rates have been steady, and the local poverty rate has increased dramatically with the recession.
>
> White House Council for Community Solutions. *Case Studies of Effective Collaboratives*. 2011. http://www.serve.gov/new-images/council/pdf/comm_collabs_case_studies.pdf

- Alignment of resources toward what works: using data to adapt continually. Regardless of their breadth, successful collaboratives pursue a logical link among the goals they seek, the interventions they support, and what they measure to assess progress and success. Collaboratives are required to be adaptive, adjusting their approaches based on new information, changes in conditions, and data on progress toward goals. At times, collaboratives may push for new services to fill in gaps. But much of the work of successful collaborations focuses

- on "doing better without spending more," or getting funders, nonprofits, government, and business to align existing resources and funding with the most effective approaches and services to achieve their goals. In many cases, this will mean working together to target efforts toward particular populations, schools, or neighborhoods rather than operating in a more ad hoc manner.

- Dedicated staff capacity and appropriate structure: linking talk to action. Having dedicated staff is critical to success, as is having a staff structure appropriate to the collaborative's plan and goals. There is no predetermined right size. Effective staff teams can range from one full-time strategic planning coordinator to as many as seven staff for more complex, formalized operations. In general, dedicated resources focus on convening and facilitating the collaborative, data collection, communications, and administrative functions.

- Sufficient funding: targeted investments to support what works. Collaboratives require funding both to maintain their dedicated staff and to ensure that nonprofits have the means to deliver high-quality services. Even though the first job of most collaboratives is to leverage existing resources, in every needle-moving collaborative studied, there was at least a modest investment in staff and infrastructure. This investment often included in-kind contributions of staff or other resources from partners. Sustainable funding itself becomes one of the collaborative's key objectives, as does "funder discipline"– sticking with the plan rather than developing individualized approaches or continuing to fund activities that are not part of the strategy.

Community Collaborative Success: Reducing Violence

Operation Safe Community, a local government-led collaborative, reduced violent crime by 27 percent and property crime by 32 percent over five years. The city of Memphis, Tennessee, struggled with violent crime in 2006, and ranked number one in the nation. Operation Safe Community was launched by the district attorney to bring law enforcement and other sectors together to address the issue by setting specific goals, establishing baseline data, and developing detailed plans in 15 areas. As a result, the murder rate is the lowest in 30 years.

White House Council for Community Solutions. *Case Studies of Effective Collaboratives.* 2011. http://www.serve.gov/new-images/council/pdf/comm_collabs_case_studies.pdf

SUPPORTIVE RESOURCES

The concept of collective impact has been growing over a number of years. However, when members of The Bridgespan Group convened leaders in collaboration, they pointed to several gaps in knowledge and tools.

Building on the substantive work of pioneering collaborative efforts that launched the evolving field of collective impact, the Council chose to focus its efforts on these gaps: life stages of a community collaborative; best practices within each stage; dedicated capacity required for success (in terms of staff time and talent, committees, oversight, etc.); and best practices in community engagement for greater impact.

As a result of these articulated needs, the Council developed specific tools and a set of 12 case studies of collaboratives that have demonstrated change for all communities interested in launching or enhancing existing collaborative efforts. These resources are available at www.serve.gov.

Community Collaborative Success: Improving Elementary Test Scores

Parramore Kidz Zone (PKZ), a neighborhood-based education collaborative, resulted in a 15 percentage point jump in reading and 21 percentage point jump in math for elementary students performing at or above grade level. Parramore was Orlando's toughest neighborhood when Buddy Dyer became the city's mayor in 2003. Data painted a bleak picture of the 1.4-square-mile neighborhood adjacent to downtown Orlando. Percentages of elementary students scoring at or above grade level on the FCAT, Florida's standardized test, were 45 percent in English and 27 percent in math in 2007. Mayor Dyer provided effective leadership and governance by aligning resources toward what worked and treating the community as partners in determining strategies to address this issue. PKZ now uses community feedback and survey results to design programming. Another key to PKZ's success is the use of data to drive the agenda. PKZ now uses teen pregnancy rates, reading and math proficiency scores, readiness for school by kindergarten indicators, and juvenile arrest rates to gauge its progress and direct its efforts.

Both reading and math scores have improved dramatically to 60 percent and 48 percent, respectively. And while Orlando's overall juvenile crime rate declined by an impressive 67 percent from 2006 to 2010, Parramore showed significantly better results with an 81 percent reduction.

White House Council for Community Solutions. *Case Studies of Effective Collaboratives.* 2011. http://www.serve.gov/new-images/council/pdf/comm_collabs_case_studies.pdf

FOCUS ISSUE: OPPORTUNITY YOUTH

★ ★

The Council focused on opportunity youth as the issue of critical national importance where the complexity and urgency of the problem requires coordinated effort to make meaningful progress. In applying the framework of successful community collaboratives to the problem, the Council first conducted research to better understand this population of young people.

UNDERSTANDING OPPORTUNITY YOUTH IN OUR NATION TODAY

The number of opportunity youth is large and diverse. As the nation strives to boost our economic competitiveness—and to put every American on a path to success—too many young adults (one out of six) are disconnected from education and work.

- In the summer of 2011, the unemployment rate of youth 16 to 24 years old was more than 18 percent or twice the overall unemployment rate; for young African Americans and Hispanics it was 30 percent and 20 percent, respectively.[1]

- Opportunity youth represent diverse socioeconomic backgrounds. While being disconnected is both a consequence and cause of poverty, many of these young people come from families of moderate means. In fact, while three out of five opportunity youth reported that they grew up in a poor or working class family, the other two said their families were middle class or better.

Youth are ready and eager to be a part of the solution. Council listening sessions and United Way Opportunity Community Conversations found that disconnected young people are assets and need to be supported to address their challenges, but are often not engaged by decision-makers. These youth want to be actively involved in developing solutions for themselves. A recent report, *Opportunity Road: The Promise and Challenge of America's Forgotten Youth*, by Civic Enterprises and America's Promise Alliance in association with Peter D. Hart Research Associates, confirmed the Council's findings. This study included in-person interviews with 613 disconnected youth in 23 locations across the United States in August 2011. Survey respondents were between the ages of 16 and 24, in numbers representative of the population as a whole in terms of gender and race/ethnicity who are currently out of school, out of work for at least six months, have no college degree, are not disabled, not incarcerated, and are not a stay-at-home parent with a working spouse.[2] Key findings included:

- Opportunity youth are optimistic. Despite their challenges, 73 percent are very confident or hopeful about achieving their goals, 85 percent want a good career and job, 67 percent want a college or technical degree, and 65 percent have a goal to finish high school or college and know they can achieve it.

- Opportunity youth accept responsibility for their futures. Some 77 percent believe that getting a good education and job are their own responsibilities.

---

1 Belfield, Clive R., Henry M. Levin, and Rachel Rosen (2012). *The Economic Value of Opportunity Youth*. Washington, DC: Civic Enterprises.

2 Bridgeland, John M. and Jessica A. Milano (2012). *Opportunity Road: The Promise and Challenges of America's Forgotten Youth*. Washington, DC: Civic Enterprises and America's Promise Alliance.

★ ★

- Opportunity youth want to reconnect to work, school, and service, but they need help.

  » The top obstacles that youth face to reconnecting to work are as follows: no jobs are available where they live (51 percent), or they don't have enough work experience (50 percent) or education (47 percent) to get the job they want. But nearly one-third (32 percent) said that they do not know how to prepare a resume or how to interview.

  » The top obstacles to reconnecting to school are as follows: cost is more than they or their families can afford (63 percent); they need to make money to take care of their families (48 percent); and they do not have transportation or they need to work and cannot balance work and school (40 percent in each case). Nearly one-third (32 percent) say no one showed them how to apply to college or helped them figure out how to pay for it.

- Opportunity youth point the way to reconnecting. Some 79 percent want to connect with successful peers they can relate to, to college professors (69 percent), and to business mentors (65 percent) to get help going back to school and work; 78 percent want job opportunities that enable them to earn some money and attend school at the same time ("Learn and Earn").

- Opportunity youth want to improve life for others. Nearly seven in ten (69 percent) want to make a difference improving life for others, while only 3 percent report they are volunteering in their communities, suggesting their disconnection from school and work is impeding their desire to give back.

These young people offer an opportunity for an infusion of potential leadership and productivity in our workforce and economy—and they are eager to accept this responsibility.

The cost of inaction is high. The need for broad national action and collaboration among business, nonprofit, and community leaders is urgent. Consider that in 2011 alone, taxpayers shouldered more than $93 billion to compensate for lost taxes and direct costs to support young people disengaged from both education and work. In their analysis *The Economic Value of Disconnected Youth*, researchers found that, over the lifetime of this group, the cost to society is estimated to be $4.7 trillion.

- Lifetime earnings are diminished with each missed year of work equating to two to three percent less earnings each year thereafter. And significant gaps in the education-work sequence of activity lead to pay and employability handicaps.

- Over a lifetime, an opportunity youth's earnings are estimated to be $375,000 compared with a high school graduate's of $712,000.[1]

---

1 Bell, David N.F. & Blanchflower, David G., 2011. *Youth Unemployment in Europe and the United States*, IZA Discussion Papers 5673, Institute for the Study of Labor (IZA).; Thomas A. Mroz & Timothy H. Savage, 2006. *The Long-Term Effects of Youth Unemployment*, Journal of Human Resources, University of Wisconsin Press.

There is opportunity to make a real impact. In addition to the value of getting these young people back on the road to successful lives, our country is facing a large skills gap that can be addressed partially by tapping the potential of this cohort of Americans. Nearly two-thirds of job openings in the next decade will require some postsecondary education.[1] To fill these jobs, the United States will need to accelerate its progress and produce three million more students who graduate with a postsecondary degree by the end of this decade.[2] Furthermore, to achieve the President's goal to lead the world in postsecondary attainment by the end of this decade, we need to produce eight million more graduates than we currently expect to produce.

UNDERSTANDING THE NEEDS OF OPPORTUNITY YOUTH

In beginning its work, the Council did extensive outreach and research to understand the demographics, needs, and existing programs for opportunity youth. The following visual (Exhibit 2) provides a snapshot of the diversity of this population in terms of their degree of preparation for, as well as their ability to take up, opportunities.

> All the solutions don't come from the programs themselves, they really come from all of the support systems, and we need everybody on board. We need the parents, we need the friends, we need the entire community.
>
> *– Maurice Miller*
> *Founder and CEO, Family Independence Initiative*

---

1 Carnevale, A.P., Smith, N. & J. Strohl. 2010. *Help Wanted. Projections of Jobs and Education Requirements through 2018.*

2 Ibid.

Exhibit 2: Opportunity Youth Segmentation

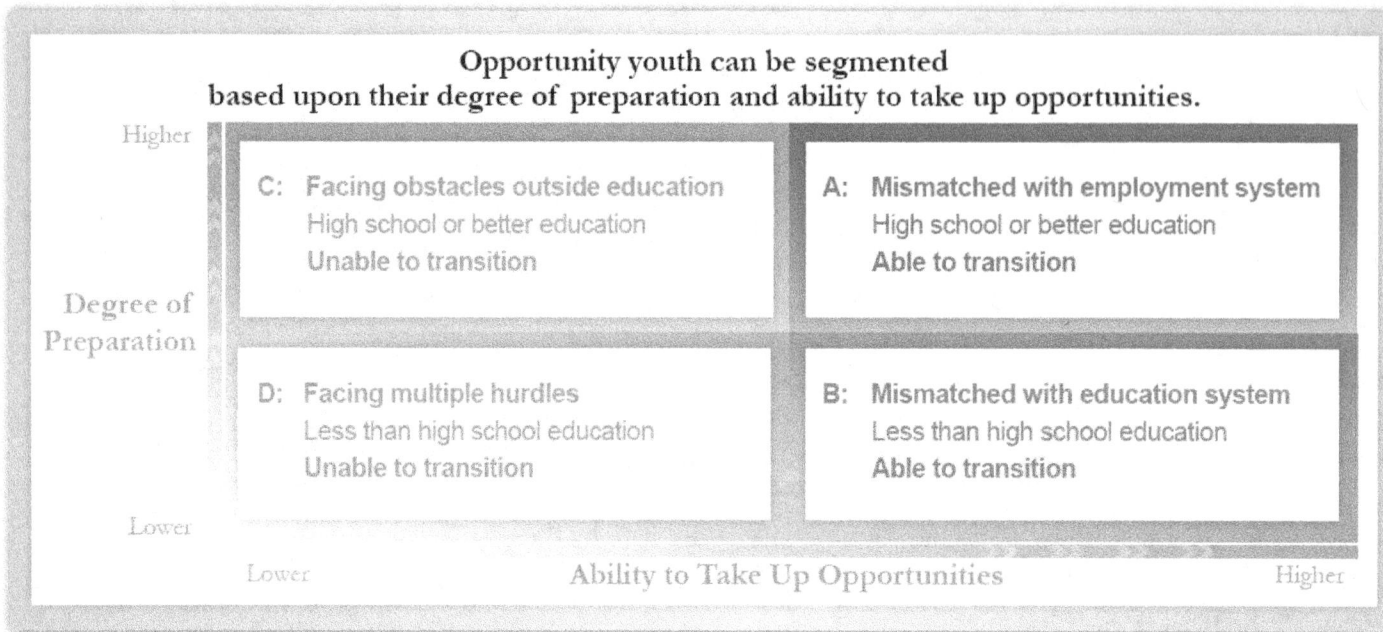

Opportunity youth can be segmented based upon their degree of preparation and ability to take up opportunities.

Higher

Degree of Preparation

Lower

C: Facing obstacles outside education
High school or better education
Unable to transition

A: Mismatched with employment system
High school or better education
Able to transition

D: Facing multiple hurdles
Less than high school education
Unable to transition

B: Mismatched with education system
Less than high school education
Able to transition

Lower — **Ability to Take Up Opportunities** — Higher

Exhibit 3: Needs and Supports Required
(Illustrates how the diversity of needs translates to a wide variety of individualized support required.)

The needs of opportunity youth are diverse and we must meet them 'where they are' ...

Types of employment opportunities open to youth increase along this spectrum

	GROUP D Facing multiple hurdles	GROUP C Facing obstacles outside education	GROUP B Mismatched with education system	GROUP A Mismatched with employment system
Critical Needs	• Integrated services across education, social supports, and employability	• Wraparound supports • Alternative pathways to learning & employment	• Pathways to GED/high school completion • Alternative training and credentialing programs	• Employment pathways & more advanced credentialing opportunities
Types of Support Required	• Opportunity for education within a stable set of interventions (Group C needs) • Move youth a step 'up the ladder' on path to full employability	• Food access • Housing & transport • Health/mental health services • Life skills mentoring • Daycare • Financial/legal literacy • Alternative pathways to GED, diploma, or community college	• High school graduation support • GED support • On the job training and work-based learning programs • Alternative credentialing programs • Afterschool/summer programs	• Community college collaborations • Certification/ credentialing programs • Internship or apprenticeship opportunities • Starter jobs

White House Council for Community Solutions

In summary, the number of opportunity youth is large, and the impact of their status is not only on the individual, but also on the nation and requires an all-in effort to make progress. While both prevention and intervention are critical to the solution, the Council focused its efforts on those already disconnected as they are often overlooked and have great potential. The needs of opportunity youth are complex and diverse, thus the solutions require a multi-sector approach to create multiple paths of opportunity to reconnect.

FUNDAMENTAL PRINCIPLES UNDERLYING RECOMMENDATIONS

Through its research, the Council developed three fundamental principles to guide all strategies addressing the needs of opportunity youth:

1. **Young people themselves are key to the solution.** Research shows that opportunity youth have informed views of what works for them and their peers.

2. **All sectors must pull together in the same direction to address the challenge.** The barriers facing opportunity youth are complex and cannot be solved by families, communities, schools, employers, nonprofits, or the government alone. To see dramatic, measurable progress in the lives of opportunity youth requires the engagement of all sectors pulling together in the same direction to provide the diverse range of services needed.

3. **Policies and funding must be data-driven to ensure limited resources are invested wisely.** Policy and funding decisions need to be guided by accurate data about opportunity youth and effective interventions to meet their needs and challenges to ensure the most effective use of limited funding.

CORE STRATEGIES
AND RECOMMENDATIONS

★ ★

Opportunity youth reside throughout our nation. Without support from individuals, community leaders, and government, they may fail to bridge to successful careers and civic lives that will improve their own futures as well as those of their communities and our nation. The good news is that strong examples of success exist. While not an exhaustive list, the Council believes the following four strategies and recommendations have the potential to make significant progress on community-based issues and specifically toward ensuring more of our nation's young people are on the path to prosperity:

- Drive Development of Successful Cross-Sector Community Collaboratives

- Create Shared National Responsibility and Accountability

- Engage Youth as Leaders in the Solution

- Build More Robust On-Ramps to Employment

STRATEGY ONE: DRIVE THE DEVELOPMENT OF SUCCESSFUL CROSS-SECTOR COMMUNITY COLLABORATIVES

Cross-sector community collaboratives that actually move the needle—realize at least a 10 percent change in the problem they aim to address—share a select set of attributes and must be replicated increasingly across the nation.

Research and practice have shown that reconnecting opportunity youth is difficult, if not impossible, within the bounds of a single intervention. The exception to this is when this single intervention is not really a single program, but a collaboration of services brought together around the needs of the youth.

Examples of success already mentioned in this report such as the Strive Partnership and Parramore Kidz Zone have proven that outcomes for youth can be improved dramatically if cross-sector assets are aligned around the needs of the youth. In addition to these already successful collaboratives, other early efforts are also under way. The United Way Worldwide responded to the President's call to action by convening a series of Opportunity Community Conversations. Affiliates across the country brought together diverse stakeholders to discuss how communities could address their community's opportunity youth needs and shared the results of these conversations with the Council. While many of the hopes and concerns voiced were similar across the country—safe places, access to opportunity, positive role models, or mentors—many of the communities also described unique assets that could be leveraged and made a commitment to begin collective action.

★ ★

KEY RECOMMENDATIONS

1. **Prioritize Funding for Best Practice Cross-Sector Community Collaboratives.** Public and private funders should prioritize successful collaborative efforts that exhibit best practice characteristics. We *strongly support the $20 million Disconnected Youth Initiative proposed in the President's 2013 budget.* The departments of Education, Health and Human Services, and Labor are proposing a total of $20 million to develop interagency strategies to strengthen the impact of federal programs serving opportunity youth and identify opportunities for enhanced flexibility and collaboration. This initiative would take the lessons from the administration's Promise Neighborhood and Choice Neighborhood initiatives that support place-based collaborative activities in communities across the country, as well as from other collaborative efforts such as the Department of Justice and Department of Education's National Forum on Youth Violence Prevention, and adapt the work to promote collaborative work focused specifically on opportunity youth.

2. **Promote Collaborative Use of Data Across Agency Lines.** Given that the ability to access and share data across systems is critical to successful solutions for complex social issues, the administration should allow local communities access to critical data across the continuum of a young person's life, improve the connection between federal, state, and local data sources, and provide clarity about the ability to share data. This increased access must be consistent with the intent of relevant privacy laws and ensure the responsible use of data. We recommend that the administration:

   » Align funding for state and local data systems. The administration should *encourage states and localities to provide more flexibility in existing programs to build, adopt, or adapt data systems and to connect disparate data collection efforts that receive federal funding.*

   » *Propose changes to the Family Educational Rights and Privacy Act (FERPA).* FERPA was written originally before personal computers were invented, and it now creates barriers to the responsible use of data across agency lines. We applaud the Department of Education's new guidance interpreting the FERPA legislation and call on the administration to go further by recommending changes to the legislation itself. More immediately, relevant agencies and their privacy attorneys should provide more helpful guidance, promising practices, and tools (i.e., sample memorandums of understanding and consent forms) for sharing data among agencies for opportunity youth.

3. **Align Policies to Reduce Fragmentation, Improve Efficiency, and Achieve Better Results.** Communities often have multiple, fragmented efforts to address complex issues, each governed by a separate federal policy that makes it difficult to align services into a coherent strategy. The administration should *simplify and align eligibility criteria, uses of funds, and reporting requirements across programs and agencies to allow coordination of services.* We applaud the President's Memorandum on Administrative Flexibility and strongly support the $113 million Performance Partnership Pilots for Disconnected Youth proposed in the President's 2013 budget. These pilots should improve outcomes for opportunity youth by supporting state, regional, or local efforts to align funding

1. from several different federal sources into coherent, efficient, and effective paths to prosperity. Pilot sites will be given the flexibility from federal regulations necessary to work across agency lines to achieve better efficiency. In areas where pilots are successful, this flexibility should be made widely available.

2. **Create a National Community of Practice.** The nonprofit sector should *establish a community of organizations dedicated to identifying and sharing best practices and developing tools for organizations committed to creating opportunities for opportunity youth.* With focused thought leadership, success could be more easily leveraged and replicated.

3. **Replicate Successful Aspects of Youth Opportunity Grants.** From 2000 to 2005, the Workforce Investment Act's (WIA) Youth Opportunity (YO) grants funded 36 high poverty rural and urban communities and Indian reservations to improve education and labor market outcomes for youth between 14 and 21 years old. YO sites brought education, job training, and wrap-around support services together in a safe, accessible youth community center. An independent evaluation of the more than 90,000 youth participants, released by the U.S. Department of Labor in 2008, found that, while results varied significantly by location and by subgroup, employment impacts were positive for most groups, especially younger youths, blacks, and native-born youths. YO also had a positive impact overall on increasing the percentage of the youth population with at least an 11th-grade education and increasing the percentage in secondary school. We recommend that the administration *encourage funding the successful aspects of YO through WIA.*

4. **Create an Incentive Fund.** The administration should *allow for the use of existing WIA formula funding to create a pilot collective impact fund* for communities that are committed to aligning existing community resources and setting specific targets to reconnect young people to school and work. This fund would be open to all proven programs and provide local communities with $1 million to $1.5 million for three years, to be matched at the local level, with resources to support data collection and other infrastructure for the community collaborative.

The Council believes enacting these recommendations will lead to a significant reduction in the population of opportunity youth through the replication of needle-moving community collaborations focused on their needs.

STRATEGY TWO: CREATE SHARED NATIONAL RESPONSIBILITY AND ACCOUNTABILITY

Shared national responsibility for opportunity youth requires high-level consistent leadership to coordinate efforts across agencies and the collection, reporting, and sharing of rigorous data to shine a national spotlight on who these young people are, what they need, and what they are capable of doing. Shared accountability also requires a clear understanding of available public and private efforts to allocate limited resources to those programs with the greatest return on investment.

As demonstrated in the core principles of successful collaboratives, to create significant progress against a complex social issue, it is critical to create a sense of shared responsibility and accountability from all sectors. Key to creating shared responsibility and accountability are long-term commitment and a data-driven shared vision.

President Bill Clinton created the President's Crime Prevention Council to coordinate federal efforts in support of at-risk youth. President George W. Bush created a White House Task Force for Disadvantaged Youth. President Obama created the White House Council for Community Solutions. To make significant progress on the issue of opportunity youth, there needs to be sustained leadership to coordinate efforts across agencies and to collect, report, and share rigorous data to shine a national spotlight on who these young people are, what they need, and what they are capable of doing.

The ability to understand the reach of an issue and have a consistent commonly defined metric against which to measure progress is essential to making progress on complex social issues. Because there is not a standard definition for this population, and there is not a single statistic or a report that is regularly published in our nation, opportunity youth remain a population below the radar for most national and community leaders and the public. In other countries such as Australia and the United Kingdom, data on so-called NEETs (Not in Education, Employment or Training) has been collected and reported for more than a decade.

With high-level consistent leadership on this issue and a publicly tracked, common metric, it will be possible to assess the range of services supporting opportunity youth and their efficacy, which is essential to creating a coordinated, cost-effective effort to make significant progress.

KEY RECOMMENDATIONS

1. **Establish High-level Consistent Leadership.** The need for senior-level prioritization, coordination, and accountability has been demonstrated in recent presidencies. Rather than recreating the function ad hoc in every new administration, we recommend that the federal government *establish an ongoing function, possibly within the Domestic Policy Council, and charge this leadership with creating goals and clarifying responsibilities among agencies for improving outcomes for opportunity youth.* The Council applauds the Department of Education's creation of the Interagency Forum on Disconnected Youth along with the existing efforts of many coordinating bodies including the Interagency Working Group for Youth Programs and the Coordinating Council on Juvenile Justice and Delinquency Prevention. Their work would be better coordinated through a single entity anchored by an annual strategy. This strategy should encompass all efforts on behalf of opportunity youth, set clear goals, and detail how federal resources will be coordinated to achieve these goals.

2. **Lead With Data.** To create greater national, state, and local accountability for reconnecting opportunity youth and to empower communities with the information they need to drive change, the administration should *begin collecting and reporting information regularly on opportunity youth through the Current Population Survey or American Community Survey.* Such information should include the size of this population, demographics, and activities.

3. **Evaluate Current Programs.** To understand the role that the federal government itself plays in reconnecting youth to education and work, the administration should *conduct a comprehensive survey across departments and agencies to understand what programs and initiatives are serving opportunity youth, how effectively they reconnect youth to education or employment, and at what scale,* perhaps through the Interagency Forum on Disconnected Youth. This evaluation can be used to allocate existing funding to the most effective programs.

4. **Scale Up and Reward Effective Programs.** The fastest way to reconnect opportunity youth is to *support effective programs that have waiting lists of young people eager to transform their lives, but for whom no slots are available.* We encourage the administration to support and Congressional leaders and state and local governments to respond by scaling successful evidence-based programs. The administration should also encourage scaling of successful programs through establishing selection criteria for Pay for Success proposals serving opportunity youth. The innovative Pay for Success funding model provides programs with a guaranteed predetermined amount of funding if they achieve agreed-upon outcomes for the populations they are serving.

5. **Invest in Innovation.** We applaud the administration's Investing in Innovation Fund, Social Innovation Fund, and Workforce Innovation Fund, and we urge the administration to *establish selection criteria for proposals serving opportunity youth and to open eligibility to nonprofit programs.*

STRATEGY THREE: ENGAGE YOUTH AS LEADERS IN THE SOLUTION

Engaging youth as leaders in developing and highlighting solutions that work will create more relevant, higher quality, and increasingly effective programs and resources for opportunity youth.

Youth want their voices to be heard, and they have strong, informed opinions of what will help them reconnect. Young people have a critical stake in the quality and sustainability of the solution as the Council heard in youth roundtables, United Way Community Conversations, and the national survey as presented in *Opportunity Road*[1].

Specifically:

- Almost 80 percent of opportunity youth want to connect with mentors to whom they can relate, such as successful peers, business mentors, and college mentors.

- Opportunity youth are more likely to respond to reconnection strategies that provide strong, integrated supports and treat youth as part of the solution rather than the problem.

There are many examples of how youth leadership has made programs more effective, including youth-driven solutions in the Chicago public school system and the Nashville Child and Youth Master Plan (see details in sidebars on pages 27 and 28).

When youth are involved as community leaders, the decisions are more relevant, reliable, and more likely to be embraced by them. Perhaps most importantly, their innate understanding of their generation allows them to develop more authentic solutions to the issues they face.

Youth as Leaders in the Solution: Higher Graduation Rates

Nashville, Tennessee has raised high school graduation rates by more than 20 percentage points to 83 percent and reduced truancy by 35 to 40 percent. Youth were involved on every level of this effort, through the youth co-chaired **Child and Youth Master Plan Task Force**, providing unique insight into solutions. Like many cities, Nashville had an array of programs and initiatives providing services and activities for children and youth, but high school graduation rates hovered around 58 percent, and school attendance was dismal. In February 2010, Mayor Karl Dean, the Mayor's Office of Children and Youth, and community leaders convened a task force to pull together the key people and organizations involved with youth in Nashville—schools, government agencies, businesses, nonprofits, youth, and parents. The Master Plan Task Force organized all youth-focused efforts into a framework and created a shared vision for the community. Using strategies from the Ready by 21 Coalition, the plan articulates desired outcomes for all children and youth for a successful future and acts as a blueprint for people and organizations to work together. Youth and their families were engaged throughout the process, and the Task Force was co-chaired by a senior from a local high school.

White House Council for Community Solutions. *Case Studies of Effective Collaboratives.* 2011. http://www.serve.gov/new-images/council/pdf/comm_collabs_case_studies.pdf

---

1 Bridgeland, John M. and Jessica A. Milano (2012). *Opportunity Road: The Promise and Challenges of America's Forgotten Youth.* Washington, DC: Civic Enterprises and America's Promise Alliance.

KEY RECOMMENDATIONS

1. Formalize Youth Input.

» Create a Presidential Youth Working Group. We applaud existing efforts to reflect youth input in the administration via the White House Liaison to Young Americans and the recent White House Young America Series. The administration should expand on these efforts and *establish a Presidential Youth Working Group composed of young people that reflects a diversity of backgrounds and experience, including opportunity youth, to advise the President and his cabinet secretaries on the perspectives of young people*, offer input on how to make federally funded youth programs more effective, and support activities by each department to better engage young people in the policy-making process.

» Call on Leading Organizations in the Nonprofit and Faith-based Sectors to Create a National Youth Council. We applaud coordinating efforts of existing organizations and collaborations to provide youth input into creating more effective nonprofit programming. To ensure youth input is specifically and consistently incorporated, *the Council calls for the expansion of an existing effort, or the creation of a new national youth council*, in addition to creating the Presidential Youth Working Group.

» Incorporate Youth Input Into Program Development and Evaluation. Nonprofit organizations (and foundations that support them) should *incorporate authentic youth input in the design and evaluation of programs and services for opportunity youth*. Specifically, nonprofits are encouraged to conduct constituency/beneficiary surveys of programs when assessing effectiveness and quality.

1. **Create an Online, Youth-Rated Service Directory.** Social sector and faith-based leaders in every community should expand an existing or create a new community-wide service inventory, youth networking and/or customer feedback tool that youth can use to assess the quality and availability of local support services. We applaud http://www.FindYouthInfo.gov, and we encourage the administration to increase its efforts and challenge the nonprofit sector to *identify a third party to extend the reach of the information in http://www.FindYouthInfo.gov and to incorporate the ability for youth to rate and recommend listings.*

2. **Hire Opportunity Youth in Program Roles.** To create more relevant youth programs and reduce stigma mistakenly attached to opportunity youth, all programs that serve youth—government, business, nonprofit, faith-based, cross sector, etc.—should *assess which of their program and advocacy needs can be filled directly by the youth they aim to serve.* The Council suggests that the Interagency Working Group on Youth Programs may be appropriate to undertake this assessment for the federal government.

We believe implementation of these recommendations will dramatically improve the efficacy of programs serving opportunity youth.

> It's values, it's attitude, it's security, it's stability. All the things that young people, our own kids need, these kids need. And they're sitting here telling you what the outcomes could be if you give them a chance. If you provide them with the resources, they'll do the rest of the work.
>
> *– Bill Strickland*
> *Founder and CEO, Manchester Craftman's Guild*

STRATEGY FOUR: BUILD MORE ROBUST ON-RAMPS TO EMPLOYMENT

Opportunity youth can be connected to employment successfully when multiple on-ramps linked to education and employment and designed to fit their community and youth needs are available and growing.

Because the needs of opportunity youth are diverse, it is necessary to meet them where they are by offering multiple on-ramps to employment—including education and service with job readiness training. Building on the Harvard Graduate School of Education's report *Pathways to Prosperity,* the PACE report *Civic Pathways Out of Poverty and Into Prosperity,* and Civic Enterprises' *Opportunity Road*, the Council's research pointed to opportunities to expand existing on-ramps and to build more robust on-ramps by increasing awareness of and access to wrap-around supports that will put youth on a path to reconnection.

The Council focused on three key engagement strategies that serve as on-ramps to employment for opportunity youth, listed below.

- **Direct to Employment**: Employers being actively engaged to successfully reconnect youth to employment through soft skills (e.g., communications, teamwork, time management) development, work-ready skills development, or learn and earn employment programs.

- **Relevant Education and Credentialing**: The education sector employing strategies to reconnect youth to education (secondary and postsecondary) and to help prevent disconnection through programs with accessibility and relevancy to opportunity youth needs.

- **Structured, Long-Term Service Programs**: Community and national service opportunities providing on-ramps for youth to gain work/life skills needed to reconnect to education and workforce opportunities.

The approach to reconnecting youth requires a multi-sector, all-in effort to be successful. It requires active engagement of different partners and is not a single actor with a single program. The interconnectedness of employers, education systems, and service—along with communities and nonprofits providing wrap-around supports—is critical for effective reconnection of this population. While the on-ramps are discussed separately, each is highly interconnected with the others, and all rely on a foundation of wrap-around support systems provided through organizations that serve youth.

Youth may need alternative learning models, soft or work-ready skills, flexible employment options, or overall integrated social support systems to enable them to take up opportunities. Employers, service organizations, educators, and youth service organizations can all play a role in meeting the needs of youth by collaborating in multi-sector efforts.

DIRECT TO EMPLOYMENT

Youth unemployment is higher than for other age groups. Seventeen percent (unadjusted) of youth were out of work in February 2012, with less than half of youth employed. By contrast, the unemployment rate for those 25 and older was 7.4 percent, with 61 percent employed. And the 11 percent who never graduate or obtain a GED find it even harder to find employment. The unemployment rate for those adults was 14.8 percent, compared with 9.2 percent for high school graduates.

Additionally, the existing workforce does not match the job requirements of the future. Georgetown University's Center on Education and the Workforce predicts a skills gap of approximately three million postsecondary degrees and 4.7 million postsecondary certificates by 2018. Even today, 80 percent of manufacturers report they cannot find people to fill their skilled production jobs, translating to more than 500,000 unfilled manufacturing jobs; some 53 percent of large employers and 67 percent of small business leaders report they cannot find qualified nonmanagerial employees.

Based on research of successful employer programs for opportunity youth, the Council believes every employer can play a role in creating paths to employment. Approximately 50 percent of opportunity youth surveyed indicated that they do not have enough work experience to get the kind of job they want. Employers have a great deal to offer young people to better prepare them for work and equip them with the right skills, experience, and outlook. Whether providing work-relevant soft skills through one-on-one mentoring or workshops, hosting job shadow days, or providing youth with an opportunity to learn on the job and develop marketable skills while receiving compensation, employers can make a difference in creating opportunities to help youth get back on track.

> **Benefits for Employers**
>
> **Johns Hopkins Health System** provides work readiness and job skills training to low-skilled, entry-level workers (and others interested) through courses taught at the hospital. Through reduction in employee turnover, the program has generated a 79 percent return on investment, and Hopkins can adjust the curriculum based on its needs.
>
> ---
>
> Corporate Voices for Working Families. *Building the Business Case for Investing in Tomorrow's Workforce: Employers See Positive Returns from Community Partnerships.* 2011.

In addition to the impact on the youth, there is a clear benefit to employers who thoughtfully develop programs for opportunity youth. Employers have reported increases in employee engagement, customer loyalty, and employee retention. These programs also provide employers with an improved local talent pipeline, help further diversity objectives, and contribute to the societal benefits of stronger communities as a whole.

Ways Employers Can Engage: The Three Lanes

Based on nationwide stakeholder listening sessions and extensive case study analysis of employers operating successful youth programs, the Council developed a set of best practices for employer engagement. These include establishing clear youth selection criteria, creating flexible education support, and providing on-the-job learning along with working with a nonprofit partner, setting high expectations, and ensuring wrap-around services are available. Building on this research, the Council identified three fundamental lanes of engagement through which a business can support youth: developing soft skills; developing work-ready skills; and offering learn and earn employment opportunities.

Exhibit 4: Three Lanes of Employer Engagement

SOFT SKILLS DEVELOPMENT	WORK-READY SKILLS DEVELOPMENT	LEARN & EARN PROGRAMS
Opportunities that provide youth with work-relevant soft skills via course work and/or direct experience	Opportunities that provide youth with insight into the world of work to prepare them for employment	Opportunities for youth to develop on-the-job skills in a learning environment while receiving wages for their work
Examples: • Soft skills workshops • Employee mentors	Examples: • Job shadow days • Career exploration guidance • Job readiness training	Examples: • Paid internships with structured training and support (e.g., buddy) • Permanent positions with structured training and support (e.g., mentor)

Soft skills are critical to success in the workplace. Company employees with a few years or more of work experience can be insightful guides for opportunity youth through one-on-one mentorship, coaching sessions, and workshops. This type of support can range from medium- to long-term commitments (e.g., mentoring) to one-time events (e.g., workshops) and is the most flexible of the three lanes of engagement.

Soft Skills Program Highlight

Southwire, a manufacturer of cables and wires in Georgia, has employees work with the Carroll County schools as mentors for young students. This allows students to combine their studies with on-the-job training (and a paycheck) in its wire manufacturing plant.

Corporate Voices for Working Families. *Building the Business Case for Investing in Tomorrow's Workforce: Employers See Positive Returns from Community Partnerships.* 2011.

White House Council for Community Solutions

Experiencing the world of work close to the source, youth begin to have a better sense of what it takes to be ready for work. Employers can host job shadow days, offer career exploration guidance, and provide job readiness training. These types of **work-ready** skills programs can be sources of inspiration for a young person and can spark a focused interest in a field or area of study.

Learn and earn programs can provide opportunity youth with the best of both worlds: an opportunity to learn on the job and develop marketable skills, and an opportunity to receive compensation for their work. These programs can come in the form of internships, apprenticeships, and permanent positions, which are usually coupled with a mentor or buddy and structured training.

It is essential that employers engaging youth work closely with a nonprofit partner. Opportunity youth can have a range of challenges in their lives, and having a partner skilled in working directly with these young people can be of great value to a business. In addition to robust partnerships, measuring the results of company efforts to assess the value to the business and make the case for continuation or expansion of the program is critical.

Work-Ready Skills Program Highlight

Gap Inc. created a program called This Way Ahead (delivered in partnership through a New York-based nonprofit, The Door) to expose opportunity youth to career exploration, job readiness training, internships, and follow-up support. In this program, 80 percent of employees improved their leadership skills as a result of volunteering.

Gap, Inc.; TCC Group, December 2009. *Evaluation Report for Gap Foundation's This Way Ahead Youth Program.* http://www. bewhatspossible.com/Home/TargetCauses.aspx

Learn and Earn Program Highlight

CVS Caremark created regional learning centers to source, train, and hire entry-level workers. The program helps untapped talent enter the industry and progress along the career path by offering innovative training, career mentoring, and education encouragement. Since the program's inception, the company has doubled its retention rate and has generated a 179 percent return on investment (return relative to costs on Work Opportunity Tax Credit). CVS's research shows a 30 percent higher retention rate among employees from these learning centers.

Corporate Voices for Working Families. *Learn and Earn Micro-Business Case Series.* 2011. http://www.corporatevoices.org/our-work/pse/ micro_cases

KEY RECOMMENDATIONS

Encourage All Sectors to Increase Job Opportunities for Opportunity Youth

» The Council was honored to participate in the administration's Summer Jobs+ initiative that partnered with corporate leaders with a goal of providing 250,000 private, government, and nonprofit sector opportunities for disconnected and disadvantaged youth in the summer of 2012. We recommend the administration continue and deepen this initiative by *increasing the target for jobs and other opportunities as currently defined in Summer Jobs+ every year, encouraging the creation of more year-round opportunities in addition to summer jobs, and by expanding this initiative to include the faith-based community.* All employers should be made aware of the tools available in *Employer Tool Kit: Connecting Youth to Employment* and should be encouraged to include mutually beneficial youth employment programs as part of their corporate social responsibility strategy.

» We applaud the administration for pledging to hire more than 20,000 opportunity or disadvantaged youth through Summer Jobs+. We encourage the administration to continue and deepen this initiative by committing to increase the number of jobs each year and by providing year-round opportunities *in addition to annual summer opportunities.*

» We applaud the administration's support of the Disconnected Youth Opportunity Tax Credit, which was authorized in the American Recovery and Reinvestment Act of 2010 and provides a tax credit to employers who hire disadvantaged youth. We recommend that the administration, with the support of Congress, *continue to build on the Disconnected Youth Opportunity Tax Credit and to strengthen it by including incentives for employers to provide a range of valuable experiences from job shadowing, career awareness, mentoring or internship programs to hiring opportunity youth.*

RELEVANT EDUCATION AND CREDENTIALING[1]

Opportunity youth often lack the credentials (high school diploma, GED, technical or postsecondary education) that lead to success in life. In fact, 47 percent of opportunity youth say they lack enough education to get their ideal job.[2] Additionally, many "best-in-class" programs are still inaccessible for the majority of opportunity youth because they require prerequisite academic skills that many of these young people lack. Youth often remain disconnected because the solutions offered by many well-meaning institutions and individuals are not tied to the systems the youth are disconnected from, or even to the issues they are facing.

Effective education efforts aimed at opportunity youth are comprehensive, youth-centered, flexible, and pragmatic. Successful interventions are those that encompass a multi-sector approach and link education to social services, mental health services, employment, and/or job training. The Council believes that educational efforts to prevent disconnection and innovative programs to encourage postsecondary reconnection and completion that follow these best practices can provide additional pathways for opportunity youth.

Keeping Youth Engaged in Education

A student's decision to drop out of school is not the result of a single life event. To the contrary, issues such as poor attendance, behavior, and problems with course completion begin to manifest as early as elementary school and into middle school. Emerging proactive strategies that address dropouts focus on students in elementary and middle schools. But early identification of students at risk of disconnection is only a first step. The key to preventing disconnection is developing the capacity of public education to mitigate the risk factors and help students stay connected, graduate, and be prepared for college and careers. Communities must develop a collective commitment and belief that graduation rates

Education Solutions: Prevention

Strive, a nonprofit based in Cincinnati, has brought together more than 300 local leaders from the private, government, secondary, and postsecondary education and nonprofit sectors to drive educational progress through collective impact, resource alignment, and data-informed decision-making. Stakeholders co-developed a common agenda, evaluation standards, and a consistent communication platform with the vision of improving the education system throughout greater Cincinnati and northern Kentucky. Strive's goals directly relate to the prevention of disconnected youth by preparing every child for school; supporting children inside and outside of school; promoting academic success; and aiming to ensure that every child enrolls and succeeds in some form of postsecondary education.

Stakeholders who participate in Strive share a common agenda, but their individual activities are not uniform. Instead, participants perform coordinated activities at which they excel and which support Strive's overarching mission. All activities are informed by the shared metrics. In the four years since its inception, the program has achieved impressive successes. Stakeholders set aside their individual agendas in favor of a collective approach in order to solve this entrenched, systemic problem.

White House Council for Community Solutions. *Case Studies of Effective Collaboratives.* 2011. http://www.serve.gov/new-images/council/pdf/comm_collabs_case_studies.pdf

---

1 Bridgeland, John M. and Jessica A. Milano (2012). *Opportunity Road: The Promise and Challenges of America's Forgotten Youth*. Washington, DC: Civic Enterprises and America's Promise Alliance.

2 *Opportunity Road: The Promise and Challenges of America's Forgotten Youth.*

Educational Solutions: Youth Re-Engagement

The **Gateway to College** program allows high school dropouts to enroll in community colleges across the country to gain the competencies needed to graduate from high school while accumulating credits toward a postsecondary credential. This program, originating at the Portland Community College in Portland, Oregon, has been replicated at 29 colleges in 16 states. Students in the Gateway to College program attend classes on the college campus; they are college students. The program pays the cost of admission, fees, and books. Gateway to College uses public education funding and the college infrastructure to support the program.

In addition to providing academic support, Gateway to College offers wrap-around services to address the social and emotional needs of students. Students are provided an opportunity to learn within a small cadre of their peers and are taught by a team of instructors and resource specialists. After the first year of intensive transitional guidance to build their academic and personal skills, students join the general college student population. The program combines high expectations with personal coaching and support.

Although the Gateway to College program is relatively new, early data indicate promising results. Students who experienced poor attendance rates in high school show an increase in attendance at Gateway to College (an average rate of 82 percent.) To date, Gateway to College students have passed 72 percent of nearly 70,000 college courses with a C or better.

White House Council for Community Solutions. *Case Studies of Effective Collaboratives.* 2011. http://www.serve.gov/new-images/council/pdf/comm_collabs_case_studies.pdf

can improve through the early, data-driven identification of potentially disconnected students, the application of diverse multi-sector strategies to address student needs, and a public education system with the capacity to provide them.

Re-engaging Opportunity Youth in Education

Innovative secondary programs, as well as postsecondary institutions, can be critical in re-engaging youth in education. Alternative GED programs and charter schools that allow for internships or other work connections are examples of how secondary education programs can be more engaging for opportunity youth.

Increasingly, colleges and universities across the nation—many of which are anchor institutions in their communities—are getting more involved in their communities and interested in the topic of youth development and alternative education. By virtue of their missions, community colleges are uniquely positioned to provide pathways to success for opportunity youth. The federal government's emphasis on and support of community colleges has the potential to provide many more opportunities for youth. Community colleges can play a critical role in re-engaging opportunity youth by providing programs for remediation and career-oriented, competency-based instruction. When they partner with other leaders from the educational and social sectors, community colleges have even greater potential to positively impact at-risk youth.

Bridging the Gap Between Education and Employment

One innovative type of educational program, a bridge program, is designed to create comprehensive pathways for youth to and through postsecondary programs and/or employment opportunities, bridging the students' experience from high school to postsecondary education or from postsecondary education to employment. Successful bridge programs incorporate strategic partnerships with education leaders at the secondary and postsecondary levels, as well as the employment and social sectors. Such partnerships allow students to access bridge programs through a variety of avenues, gain knowledge and experience that is relevant to their career aspirations, and receive guidance on a range of topics and issues.

In addition, these types of innovative partnerships between education and employment are critical to ensuring our youth get the type of skills our labor market is demanding. This multi-sector approach can help youth reconnect and prepare for the workforce, while equipping them with the most relevant set of skills.

Educational Solutions: Partnering With Employers

In a new study by the Manufacturing Institute (http://www.themanufacturinginstitute.org/Research/Skills-Gap-in-Manufacturing/2011-Skills-Gap-Report/2011-Skills-Gap-Report.aspx) more than 80 percent of manufacturers report they cannot find people to fill their skilled production jobs. As a result, more than 500,000 manufacturing jobs are open right now. Responding to this talent crisis and to the need to create jobs in this country, the Institute worked with the President's Jobs Council to tailor the national manufacturing certification system into a nationally replicable fast-track solution to deliver just in time talent to small manufacturers. This accelerated program, **Right Skills Now**, allows individuals to earn college credit and national industry certifications in 16 weeks, preparing them for immediate employment in high-quality manufacturing jobs and giving them a solid foundation to advance in higher education and careers.

Educational Solutions: Community Colleges Connecting Education to Employment

Skills for America's Future is an initiative of the Aspen Institute to create a national network of partnerships among employers, community colleges, industry associations, and other stakeholders. These partnerships are designed to ensure Americans receive the training necessary to meet the needs of employers and have the opportunity to get and keep good jobs. Since the initiative was announced in October 2010, Skills for America's Future has successfully helped create or expand partnerships between more than 30 employers and 200 community colleges across the country.

An example is Metropolitan College, a Louisville, Kentucky-based partnership between UPS, government, and postsecondary educational institutions. The program offers participants both financial support for study and part-time employment at UPS. As of 2010, 2,600 individuals, who had participated in Metropolitan College for one or more semesters, had earned 3,760 credentials including 1,024 certificates, 966 associate's degrees, 1,576 bachelor's degrees, and 194 advanced degrees. In addition to benefits for participants, Metropolitan College has dramatically stabilized UPS's overnight workforce and provided reliable, skilled employees to staff UPS operations in Louisville.

KEY RECOMMENDATIONS

Provide High-Quality, Relevant Educational Opportunities for Opportunity Youth

» *We applaud the administration's Blueprint for Investing in America's Future: Transforming Career and Technical Education* (CTE) and in particular its four core principles: alignment, collaboration, accountability, and innovation. The administration's proposal would use a combination of technical assistance, competition, and a system of structured rewards to ensure that more students, regardless of backgrounds or circumstances, have access to high-quality CTE programs. The current act provides separate funding streams for local education agencies and postsecondary institutions, making alignment challenging, and weakening a student's ability to transition between secondary and postsecondary systems. The administration's proposal would discontinue this approach by requiring states to competitively fund consortia of Local Education Agencies (LEAs), postsecondary institutions, and their partners. The proposal includes provisions to ensure competitive funding has no adverse impact on access for vulnerable student populations including, for instance, the authority for states to establish absolute funding priorities. The proposal would also require that at least one of the LEAs in the consortia serve a high concentration of students from low-income families and allow resources for states to provide services for opportunity youth.

» We applaud the Department of Education's Together for Tomorrow initiative to involve faith-based and other community organizations in developing and supporting programs that increase school attendance, improve behavior, support academic achievement, and increase college accessibility. We recommend the administration encourage the postsecondary education community to *scale effective examples of community- and faith-based organizations to provide opportunity youth the remediation, support services, and career-oriented instruction necessary for their success.*

» The administration should *encourage the K-12 system to do more data-driven early identification and prevention of school disconnection.* Specifically, early warning information and intervention systems should be put in place in schools to identify those students whose attendance, behavior, and course completion records signal the need for school-based and community-based supports. These systems should be combined with appropriate programs for recovery.

» Encourage school districts and community and faith-based organizations to provide high-quality remedial and dropout recovery services to opportunity youth. Current offerings are not sufficient to meet the need. Regulations should *encourage dropout recovery services, and Race to the Top should include selection criteria for applicants including reconnecting opportunity youth strategies in their state plans.*

» We applaud the administration's support of Skills for America's Future, an industry-led initiative to improve industry partnerships with community colleges and build a nationwide network to maximize workforce development strategies, job training programs, and job placements. We recommend that the administration *continue its support of efforts that meet the needs of local employers in today's dynamic economy.*

★ ★

» We recommend the administration *encourage the military and employers to work closely with higher education institutions to align work experience with curriculum for degree-granting programs* to allow those participating in qualifying military and employer training or work experiences to earn academic credit.

STRUCTURED, LONG-TERM SERVICE PROGRAMS

A structured, long-term service program is a viable path for opportunity youth to connect to postsecondary education and the workforce. In fact, nearly seven in ten (69 percent) of opportunity youth surveyed want to make a difference in the lives of others, while only three percent report that they are volunteering. This indicates that there is an untapped interest in service opportunities, and these very opportunities can provide a path to further education and employment. In fact, service has long been an on-ramp to the nonprofit field, which is one of the fastest growing occupations in our economy today.

Existing Service Programs Offer Opportunity for Youth

The roots of the modern service movement took hold during the Great Depression of the 1930s when the Civilian Conservation Corps put three million young people to work over a decade to restore the nation's parks and developing infrastructure, while allowing those young people to support themselves and their families. Today there are many opportunities for service both locally and nationally. Full-time, structured, long-term (at least six months) service programs for youth can provide a meaningful transition to either employment or education. Participants do real work helping communities address issues in education, health, poverty, housing, conservation, veterans' services, and disaster preparedness and relief.

These service programs often include program elements recognized as best practices in successfully engaging youth, including high expectations, wrap-around support, work-relevant learning opportunities, and a connected, caring adult.

Service: Connecting Opportunity Youth to Education

Support for educational achievement that service programs provide is an incentive to enroll in a service program. Such programs are also often transformational in the lives of opportunity youth. The primary educational support offered by many such service programs is the Segal AmeriCorps Education Award that is given upon completion of service and can be applied to further postsecondary expenses or to repay qualified student loans.

> ### Service as a Path to Education
>
> **AmeriCorps National Civilian Community Corps** (NCCC) partnered with the Nonprofit Leadership Alliance to create a nonprofit leadership certificate. A member's experience earns them most of the requirements for the certificate program, including fulfilling the internship requirement. AmeriCorps NCCC works closely with partner universities to enroll students in the remaining required courses. The Louisiana State University in Shreveport, for example, offers NCCC additional benefits like waiving the GRE requirement, allowing members to pay in-state tuition, and providing the option to take classes online. Graduates of NCCC also earn an educational award to apply toward future post-secondary courses.

Additionally, many service programs have a built-in academic curriculum and offer other external educational opportunities. Remedial and GED-prep courses are offered in many programs. Others offer courses in specific industries to allow members to earn nationally recognized certifications.

Service programs are taking additional steps to improve their members' educational outcomes. Some service programs are now holding education fairs, building postsecondary partnerships, including setting up college credit agreements in which participants receive undergraduate credit for completing their service programs, and providing online transition guidance for service members completing their terms.

Service: Connecting Opportunity Youth to Employment

Service As a Path to Employment

Through the **National Guard Youth ChalleNGe Program,** cadets have the opportunity to develop work-ready skills through career assessment and interest inventories, job-specific skills orientation and awareness, and training in area vocational centers. Classes cover the development of individual resumes, how to complete job applications, and what is needed to prepare for and go through a job interview. Key to success is a self-selected mentor that works with the cadet to develop a 12-month post-residential plan to help guide them after graduation. The mentor remains in contact for a full year after the cadet has completed the program, ensuring that the life plan is being followed.

In addition to encouraging educational aspirations of members, many service programs have workforce development initiatives that equip youth with essential skills they need to be contributing members in the economy and their communities. Graduates of service programs enhance their employability through acquisition of various soft skills and work-ready skills developed through specifically designed program elements geared toward enhanced employability, and a new social network.

Service programs are an especially effective pipeline for jobs in the fast-growing nonprofit sector. The nonprofit sector employs 10.5 million workers or one-tenth of all U.S. workers. It is the third largest industry behind manufacturing and retail. From 2008 to 2010, while private sector employment declined eight percent, nonprofit employment grew 4.5 percent. Because many opportunity youth have been clients of nonprofit services, their experience makes them especially prepared to be service providers and leaders on issues they know well.

Skills training is inherent in the nature of service programs. Whether it is work-ready skills such as CPR training, disaster relief, construction or health care, service programs require on-the-job training as part of the experience and many require pre-service training as well. Members also develop soft skills such as a strong work ethic, time management skills, respect for authority, self-advocacy, leadership, public speaking, flexibility, resourcefulness, and teamwork.

Furthermore, many service programs connect their members to opportunities that help their graduates transition into the workplace. Some programs conduct workshops on building resumes, teach business etiquette or provide mentors to help members develop "life plans." Mock interview sessions are also available in some programs.

These new skills translate to employment opportunities. According to a 2008 independent report, AmeriCorps VISTA members were consistently more likely to be employed than their counterparts in the comparison group. Despite similarities in career choices, VISTA members reported a higher current income profile than their counterparts in the comparison group.[1] Additionally, 67 percent of AmeriCorps state and national members and 70 percent of AmeriCorps NCCC members report that their experiences provided them with an advantage in finding a job.[2]

History has proven and programs today show evidence that service can provide a viable path for opportunity youth to education and employment. While many programs are successful today, the Council believes that it will require the service sector working more closely with the educational and employment sectors to improve and expand these on-ramps for opportunity youth.

> And through the love and respect of both of those (national service) programs, we were allowed to utilize that energy, and channel that into something that became community outreach, things that build our communities, make better leaders, and also helped in our situations.
>
> *– Kareema Barr*
> *Youth Build Graduate*

1 Corporation for National and Community Service, *Improving Lives and Communities: Perspectives on 40 Years of VISTA Service*. Washington, DC: 2008.

2 Corporation for National and Community Service, Office of Research and Policy Development, *Still Serving: Measuring the Eight-Year Impact of AmeriCorps on Alumni*. Washington, DC: 2008.

KEY RECOMMENDATIONS

1. **Increase Service Opportunities Available to Opportunity Youth and Ensure Strong Links to Education and Employment**

   » We applaud AmeriCorps National Civilian Community Corps' (NCCC) 50 percent target for disadvantaged youth members and the new Federal Emergency Management Agency/NCCC initiative that creates more service opportunities for opportunity youth. We recommend Corporation for National and Community Service (CNCS) *expand this effort by setting annual targets to increase the percentage of disadvantaged youth slots available and by establishing a cross-cutting priority for all programs that engage opportunity youth in service,* to ensure that its impact priorities do not disadvantage programs that engage such young people. Grant-based service programs should provide incentives through rewarding programs that propose and show evidence of successfully serving opportunity youth.

   » Many service programs have established evidence of success in providing an on-ramp for youth from service to education and employment. Many of these same service programs also have waiting lists. The Council *recommends that the administration support and Congressional leaders, state and local governments respond by scaling successful evidence-based service programs.*

   » We applaud the inclusion of the Opportunity Corps in the Edward M. Kennedy Serve America Act. The Council *recommends implementing this initiative to reconnect youth and enlist their help in boosting the social mobility of others in their communities.*

   » We applaud the progress being made by the 21st Century Corps Initiative in creating stronger links between corps service and successful careers. CNCS should *continue to promote stronger links to education and employment,* including elements from transition to work programs such as providing academic credits from educational institutions and certifications from training programs and focusing on critical workforce skills that can be developed through service.

2. **Help Opportunity Youth Find Mentors**

   » We applaud the administration's mentoring efforts including the First Lady's Corporate Mentoring Challenge and the Office of Juvenile Justice and Delinquency Prevention's multiple mentoring initiatives and *recommend that these efforts be expanded and deepened by encouraging youth-initiated mentoring.*

CLOSING SUMMARY

★★

Community collaboratives with specific key attributes can achieve significant improvement in a variety of persistent community issues. While a dozen of these successful collaboratives were documented through the Council's research, approximately 100 more were identified as moving in the direction of accomplishing needle-moving change. With the right tools and supports, these promising collaboratives are poised to create significant improvement in their communities.

The population of opportunity youth is large and eager to take charge of their futures, but at the same time, it has complex and diverse needs. The benefits of reconnecting these youth to education or employment are enormous and require urgent action from all sectors.

Many efforts are expanding or being initiated to drive the growth of both successful community collaboratives and solutions for opportunity youth, including the Office of Management and Budget Performance Partnership Pilots, the United Way Community Conversations, and a new Aspen Institute Forum for Community Solutions. (Please see Appendix C for more examples of new efforts under way.)

With evidence in hand and movement underfoot, the Council believes that implementing the recommendations highlighted in this report—driving the development of successful cross-sector community collaboratives, creating a nationwide awareness and accountability for opportunity youth, engaging youth as leaders in the solution, and building more robust on-ramps to employment—will lead to significant progress on solving many persistent community issues, including ensuring all of our young people are on the path to prosperity.

★★

APPENDICES

★★

★★

Appendix A:
STAKEHOLDER OUTREACH SUMMARY

★ ★

BACKGROUND

Members of the White House Council for Community Solutions engaged diverse stakeholders from across the country in meetings, roundtables, community-based listening sessions, and webinars between the months of March and May 2011. Formal listening sessions were held in New Orleans, Louisiana; Atlanta, Georgia; Houston, Texas; San Francisco, California; and Cincinnati, Ohio. This document provides a synthesis of the input collected from the more than 300 stakeholders across communities and sectors.

KEY FINDINGS: WHAT YOUNG PEOPLE NEED TO RECONNECT AND SUCCEED

PROGRAMS

*   Holistic programs, or network of services, that address a full range of needs, with additional "seats" (capacity) in existing programs that work (rather than accessing multiple programs to meet each specific need)

*   Accessible programs that are personalized and include a caring adult (mentor) and the opportunity to build social networks

*   Multiple paths to success, including a variety of on-ramps and reentry paths that meet young people where they are

*   Effective programs that address the needs of those youth performing significantly below grade level when they leave the education system (estimated to be up to 70 percent of opportunity youth)

*   High-quality, relevant education and job training programs that prepare youth for real job opportunities and better access to relevant work experience

COMMUNICATION

*   Expanded outreach to increase young peoples' awareness of programs that work

*   Elimination of stereotypes of the limitations of opportunity youth and messaging that reinforces youth as assets

PREVENTION AND INTERVENTION

*   Improvements to systems that fail youth and lead to the point of disconnection (e.g., foster care, education, juvenile justice)

*   Involvement of caring adults, (including parents and guardians, when possible) to be mentors and positive role models

*   Opportunities for positive peer support

★ ★

KEY FINDINGS: WHAT'S NEEDED FOR EFFECTIVE CROSS-SECTOR COLLABORATION

- Clearly defined problem, trust among stakeholders, community-wide common goals and metrics and data-driven decisions

- Effective design involving all stakeholders, e.g., youth, educators, employers, credentialing entities, youth-serving organizations, and other stakeholders

- Incentives for existing collaboratives to address challenges facing youth rather than formation of new collaboratives

KEY FINDINGS: WHAT STAKEHOLDERS NEED TO MOVE FORWARD

- A common language articulating the challenge, a clearly defined business case for each stakeholder, and proof that transformation is possible

- Defined opportunities to engage and add value that align with stakeholders' missions and capitalize on organizational competencies

- Better access to and alignment of public (state/local/federal) and private resources

- Engagement of noncorporate employers (e.g., local government, universities, health care, among others), particularly those with growth in job opportunities

Appendix B: UNITED WAY OPPORTUNITY COMMUNITY CONVERSATIONS

★★

BACKGROUND

United Way Worldwide planned a series of Opportunity Community Conversations to bring together people, businesses, government, and nonprofits to create real change in education, income, and health. In response to President Obama's call to action at the January 5, 2012, Summer Jobs + event, United Way Worldwide invited the Council to participate in these conversations throughout the country. This resulted in more than 125 community conversations occurring from February through March 2012.

The community conversations were hosted and managed on a voluntary basis by the local United Way affiliates, with leadership and support from United Way Worldwide. Each affiliate that participated committed to holding three to five conversations. Many of these conversations were with everyday people, and at least one conversation in each community included community leaders.

SUMMARY

Across the nation, community conversations including youth, families, adults, community, nonprofit, business, and government leaders surfaced common challenges and opportunities for addressing the needs of opportunity youth. In describing their toughest challenges, youth reported difficulty navigating and accessing local services, a dearth of mentors and role models, inadequate pathways to meaningful employment and education, and a concern for basic safety. Across communities, youth were characterized by a distrust of government, preferring to engage with local organizations. A strong entrepreneurial spirit also characterized youth, with many calling for a louder voice and a more prominent role in serving their local communities. Youth are coping with common struggles: many expressed frustration with their family unit, disillusionment with local schools and law enforcement, and disenchantment with the lack of employment opportunities tailored specifically for youth.

These findings point to great opportunity for improvement, including more collaboration between service providers, more mentors, a more individualized approach to services for youth, youth involvement in creating solutions, and greater accessibility to information about available services.

OVERVIEW OF COMMUNITY CONVERSATIONS

The Council participated in the community conversations to meet three objectives:

- To spark informed action in communities around the nation, creating solutions for disconnected youth.

- To make sure that information about opportunity youth and the tools for addressing their needs were disseminated widely to those who are in the best position to create opportunities for these youth.

- To inform the recommendations in the Council's final report to the President by gathering information on what works and on the challenges and opportunities in implementing community solutions.

The United Way affiliates invited attendees based on their network in their local communities. In addition, Council members worked with affiliates to create a mix of participants who are thought leaders and innovators in the area of collaborative efforts and opportunity youth.

The moderated discussions were framed with data from two research reports *Opportunity Road: The Promise and Challenges of America's Forgotten Youth* and *The Economic Value of Opportunity Youth.*

The discussion engaged participants in an in-depth dialogue around the following topics:

- What creates opportunities/a good life in a community?

- What is standing in the way of achieving this opportunity?

- What could be done to create these opportunities/good lives?

- Specifically with regard to opportunity youth:

   » What successful programs exist?

   » Who should be at the table to create opportunities, and what would it take to get them involved?

   » What challenges and opportunities exist in this community in addressing the needs of opportunity youth?

KEY FINDINGS

YOUTH ASPIRATIONS

Across cities and conversations, in discussing aspirations, responses are strongly consistent. First and foremost, youth want safety, a palpable sense of community engagement, a strong family unit, and a credible opportunity to realize the American dream. Youth want to live in an environment that is safe, inclusive of diversity (including differences in sexual orientation and identity), and supportive of youth and their aspirations. Along these lines, youth want to live in neighborhoods in which neighbors and community members are explicitly positive and supportive, not actively destructive or pessimistic. Youth want to enjoy an educational system that prepares them for a better future. Youth want access to meaningful employment. Critical to meaningful employment and to enjoying a meaningful future more broadly is mentorship. Youth want access to quality mentorship and exemplary role models because youth want to feel supported day-to-day and youth recognize how important mentorship is in successfully navigating an increasingly complex job and educational market.

Interestingly, a common aspiration among youth is also a strong desire to be free of government intervention and support. There is a powerful aversion to dependence on government that emerges in the conversations. However, youth consistently held high hopes for their communities and, oftentimes, respected the community organizations striving to serve them. Importantly, youth aspire to be helped by their communities, not government.

Lastly, youth aspire to serve their communities, too. Youth aspire to have a louder voice in their communities and want to play a stronger role in confronting common challenges. Youth are extremely entrepreneurial, but have few means available to them through which to exercise their pioneering spirit. While youth certainly need support and services, youth also require an opportunity to serve and to give back.

YOUTH CHALLENGES

Across the nation, youth most commonly identified the following as their most difficult challenges:

- Difficulty navigating and accessing local services. Accessing and navigating services is a challenge common among youth. Youth label services delivered by both the social sector and the government as fragmented, uncoordinated, insensitive to individual concerns, and stigmatizing. Youth are calling for services that are less stigmatizing, more individualized, and tightly integrated among providers.

- A dearth of role models and mentors. Youth are calling for more role models and mentors to help them with the difficult and often complex paths to rewarding employment and education. Traditional sources of mentorship have proven inadequate; youth are often disenchanted with local teachers, law enforcement, and even the family unit.

- Inadequate pathways to employment and education. The devastated economy and an increasingly competitive but deeply inadequate school system have taken a huge toll on youth and their prospects for opportunities. For many youth, there are few, if any, clear paths to meaningful employment or education. Youth need stronger on-ramps to paths leading to meaningful employment or education, and more guidance (e.g., mentorship) as they walk along these paths.

- Safety. A palpable sense of insecurity and danger is evident in many conversations with youth. This is compounded by the difficult relationship many youth have with local enforcement. Strengthening the relationship between youth, local law enforcement, and local government could contribute to a greater sense of well-being among youth in their communities.

WHAT NEEDS TO CHANGE?

Youth are asking for basic physical and economic security and educational and occupational opportunity. While there are organizations working to provide these things for youth, a frequent and passionate theme among adult participants was the frequency with which nonprofit and community organizations failed to coordinate, pool resources, and collaborate. Many of the adult participants cite the lack of connections among/between organizations and the negative effect that has on services to youth. Some organizations have reported creating databases of resources and referrals geared toward helping program participants. But organizations must go further.

Therefore, the prevalence of destructive turf wars was cited as a persistent theme. Many participants strongly desired a lead agency that acts as a neutral agent responsible for convening local parties; a good lead agency isn't necessarily a lead but rather a starting point for community change. Without collaboration, many youth are excluded from community services.

Youth were consistently emphatic about the need for role models and positive mentors. Simply, youth are not exposed to enough positive role models in their communities, nor are they receiving the individualized support that comes from having a mentor. Mentors are crucial to ensuring a meaningful work experience, to navigating the complex systems of public education as well as the difficulties inherent to many underserved communities.

OPPORTUNITIES AND POTENTIAL RECOMMENDATIONS

A number of possible recommendations emerged:

- Participants are calling for more collaboration among organizations to close critical gaps in services.

- Youth are calling for more role models and mentors.

- Participants are calling for organizations that effectively meet their individual needs and concerns.

- Youth are eager to be part of the solution; calls for more tutoring or peer counseling are common. However, youth report that they are rarely asked to serve their peers in their community.

- Adult participants are eager for a forum through which to better understand stakeholder concerns. Adults are often unclear as to the true needs of youth and often have no mechanism by which to surface those needs; moreover, adults are also unclear as to the mission and agenda of other organizations, and how to foster compelling collaboration.

Appendix C:
EXAMPLES OF NEW EFFORTS UNDER WAY

★★

The Council deeply appreciates the over 300 individuals and organizations that took the time to share their insights and ideas. Their counsel greatly influenced the Council's work and strengthened the recommendations in this report. The Council commends their continued commitment to supporting opportunity youth achieve their dreams.

The Council would like to acknowledge the following new efforts on behalf of opportunity youth. This list is not intended to be all-inclusive, given that many more efforts are under way or will be launched in the future.

DRIVE THE DEVELOPMENT OF SUCCESSFUL CROSS-SECTOR COMMUNITY COLLABORATIONS

ASPEN FORUM FOR COMMUNITY SOLUTIONS

The Aspen Institute is creating the Aspen Forum for Community Solutions, to be led by Melody Barnes, former assistant to the president and director of the Domestic Policy Council for President Obama, along with a senior-level executive director to drive and manage the day-to-day work. The forum will spotlight success stories, educate national and local leaders about this strategy, and provide community leaders with some of the knowledge and tools they will need to launch a successful collaborative.

The forum will focus on three key objectives:

- Engage and enlist community leaders to pull together for change.

- Provide the knowledge and tools communities need to create effective collaboratives.

- Incent more needle-moving community collaborations focused on opportunity youth through an opportunity youth incentive fund.

RECONNECTING OPPORTUNITY YOUTH – TULANE UNIVERSITY

In March 2012, the Cowen Institute for Public Education Initiatives at Tulane University launched its initiative Reconnecting Opportunity Youth. With funding support from AT&T, the Cowen Institute is examining the challenges that opportunity youth face, assessing services that are available to them currently in the Greater New Orleans area, and analyzing strategies that enable struggling youth to reach their potential and contribute to their community. Additionally, the institute is taking its findings and developing a specific community action plan to address the issue of opportunity youth in New Orleans—with the goal of creating an infrastructure of effective, sustainable, and meaningful services and programs that will prepare these young people for college and career. By sharing outcomes with the community and reaching out to key players, the Cowen Institute is laying the groundwork for collective impact. Following its call to action, the institute will initiate a citywide, multi-sector collaborative to accomplish systemic change and significantly increase the number of young New Orleanians who embark on paths that lead to careers and engaged lives.

★★

UNITED WAY OPPORTUNITY COMMUNITY CONVERSATIONS AND COMMON GOOD AWARDS

United Way Worldwide planned a series of Opportunity Community Conversations to bring together people, businesses, government, and nonprofits to create real change in education, income, and health. This resulted in more than 125 Community Conversations occurring from February through March 2012. These conversations are serving as the springboard for community-based action including new partnerships and jobs initiatives.

Additionally, United Way Worldwide launched a new effort to recognize collaboratives and partnerships that are advancing education, income, and health. The awards highlight innovative and promising practices from communities around the world that are making measurable progress in education, income and health—the building blocks for a good quality of life.

There were three overall award winners announced at the United Way Town Hall in May: The United Way Common Good Award for Advancing Education, Advancing Income, and Advancing Health. Winning community collaboratives each demonstrate a shared understanding of their community's challenges and a commitment to taking a joint approach to addressing them.

FAMILY INDEPENDENCE INITIATIVE AWARDS

The new Family Independence Initiative (FII) Award will recognize and reward groups of families, friends, and community members who have taken it upon themselves to organize and create solutions to engage and reconnect their youth to the larger community. As examples of how all communities are full of families with ideas, wisdom, and determination, honorees will inspire others to organize in their own communities.

There are numerous excellent programs that exist for young people, but often the most productive engagement for youth is with their families and friends in their communities. These everyday heroes don't work through an organization or agency; they do it on their own. They do it without the support of programs, services, or philanthropic funding. The FII Award will provide seed funding over two years to recognize four self-organized groups each year. It will also provide a venue for sharing with the nation that the seeds of change exist in our most disenfranchised communities.

OPPORTUNITY NATION INITIATIVES

Opportunity Nation (ON) is working along three key avenues to ensure ongoing progress for opportunity youth. ON will be hosting a revised and updated interactive version of *Employer Tool Kit: Connecting Youth to Employment*, as well as the *Community Collaboratives Tool Box*. It is working with Columbia University to ensure that the national data from *The Economic Value of Disconnected Youth* will be available on a community level. ON is also creating a plan of action for both public and private sectors to reach at least one million opportunity youth with efforts to reconnect them to education and employment.

Opportunity Nation is a broad coalition of nearly 200 businesses, nonprofits, educational institutions, and military organizations seeking to create a shared, bipartisan plan to create better skills, better jobs, and better communities.

ENGAGE YOUTH AS LEADERS IN THE SOLUTION

THE SPARKOPPORTUNITY CHALLENGE

The SparkOpportunity Challenge is an initiative of SparkAction in partnership with the Youth Leadership Institute and dozens of leading youth-engagement organizations across the country. During the spring of 2012, young people were encouraged to propose their own visionary yet viable solutions to create jobs, build and enhance skills, and bring about real change for opportunity youth. The approaches to create local jobs generated through this challenge have the potential to be replicated in other communities.

Participants were instructed to upload a short video and/or text description of their ideas to SparkAction's contest platform. Winners to be announced in June 2012, will receive seed grants and technology to support starting their project up, and other opportunities, such as the chance to share their ideas with CEOs, government officials, and business leaders, and to receive feedback and assistance with implementation, a promotional video featuring their ideas, and help with fund-raising. (Winners will be listed on the Challenge web site, http://sparkaction.org/sparkopportunity.)

The goal of the six-week challenge is to identify viable youth-driven solutions and to highlight the ideas and perspectives of young people. In the longer term, the challenge presents an opportunity to implement the winning ideas in communities around the country, potentially informing national strategies to improve the workforce and economy.

YOUTH LEADERSHIP INSTITUTE YOUTH AMBASSADORS

Over the past few months, the Youth Leadership Institute has recruited and trained 11 "youth ambassadors" to raise awareness and spark action on behalf of opportunity youth by serving as spokespeople in local and national forums.

The youth and young adults were selected because of their powerful personal stories about overcoming challenges to successfully engage in education and work, many of them through vital pathways that provided them with real work skills, mentors, internships, and social and financial support.

The Youth Leadership Institute created the Youth Ambassador Program as part of its effort to help bring powerful youth voices to national and community discussions inspired by the work of the White House Council for Community Solutions.

BUILD MORE ROBUST ON-RAMPS TO EMPLOYMENT

SUMMER JOBS+

Summer Jobs+ is a call to action for businesses, nonprofits, and government to work together to provide pathways to employment for low-income and disconnected youth in the summer of 2012. As of May 2012, this initiative is providing nearly 300,000 opportunities. Employment opportunities include 90,000 paid jobs and thousands of mentorships, internships, and other training opportunities. This initiative is also launching the Summer Jobs+ Bank, a new online search tool to help connect young people to jobs, internships, and other employment opportunities this summer and year-round.

SAN FRANCISCO SUMMER JOBS+ LAUNCH

Inspired by the Department of Labor's Summer Jobs+ program, San Francisco Mayor Ed Lee and United Way of the Bay Area announced the launch of San Francisco Summer Jobs+ in April 2012. The initiative aims to create 5,000 jobs and paid internships for young people this summer. It is San Francisco's local response to President Obama's national call to action for businesses, nonprofits, and government to provide pathways to employment for young people, especially low-income and disconnected youth.

A local youth employment program, MatchBridge, will take the lead in the program to support young job seekers with resources such as work-readiness workshops, resume writing assistance, interview tips, and job-search coaching. MatchBridge will also work with employers to ensure a good match with youth employees.

Appendix D:
BIBLIOGRAPHY

★★

American Youth Policy Forum (2011). *Key Considerations for Serving Disconnected Youth.*

Ashby, Cornelia M. (2008). *Disconnected Youth: Federal Action Could Address Some of the Challenges Faced by Local Programs That Reconnect Youth to Education and Employment.* Washington, DC: United States Government Accountability Office.

Bauldry, Shawn, and Tracey A. Hartmann (2004). *The Promise and Challenge of Mentoring High-Risk Youth: Findings from the National Faith-Based Initiative.* Philadelphia: Private/Public Ventures. (2004).

Bernstein, Lawrence, Catherine Dun Rappaport, Lauren Olsho, Dana Hunt, Marjorie Levin (2009). *Impact Evaluation of the US Department of Education's Student Mentoring Program.* Washington, DC: Institute of Education Sciences.

Bloom, Dan, Saskia Levy Thompson, and Rob Ivry (2010). *Building a Learning Agenda Around Disconnected Youth.* New York: MDRC.

Boisi, Geoffrey T., Haim Saban, Alan D. Schwartz, and Gail Manza (2006). *The National Agenda for Action: How to Close the Mentoring Gap.* Alexandria, VA: MENTOR.

Bozell, Maureen R., and Melissa Goldberg (2009). *Employers, Low-Income Young Adults, and Postsecondary Education Credentials: A Practical Typology for Business, Education, and Community Leaders.* Barrington, RI: Workforce Strategy Center.

Bridgeland, John M., John J. DiIulio, Jr., and Karen Burke Morrison (2006). *The Silent Epidemic: Perspectives of High School Drop-Outs.* Washington, DC: Civic Enterprises.

Bridgeland, John M., Jessica Milano, and Elyse Rosenblum (2011). *Across the Great Divide: Perspectives of CEOs and College Presidents on America's Higher Education and Skills Gap.* Washington, DC: Civic Enterprises.

Brown Lerner, J., and Betsy Brand (2006). *The College Ladder: Linking Secondary and Postsecondary Education for Success for All Students.* Washington, DC: American Youth Policy Forum.

Campaign for Youth (2008). *Our Youth, Our Economy, Our Future: A National Investment Strategy for Reconnecting America's Youth.*

Campbell-Kibler Associates (2009). *Youth Development Institute: Community Education Pathways to Success, Final Evaluation Report.*

★★

Carnevale, Anthony P., Nicole Smith, and Jeff Strohl (2010). *Help Wanted: Projections for Jobs and Education Requirements through 2018.* Washington, DC: Georgetown University Center on Education and the Workforce.

Carnavale, Anthony P., and Stephen J. Rose (2010). *The Undereducated American.* Washington, DC: Georgetown University Center on Education and the Workforce.

Corporate Voices for Working Families (2007). *Business Leadership: Supporting Youth Development and the Talent Pipeline.*

Corporation for National and Community Service (2006). *AmeriCorps NCCC Fact Sheet.*

Corporation for National and Community Service (2008). *Nonprofit CEOs Hail AmeriCorps as Source for Future Leaders, Press Release.*

Communities Collaborating to Reconnect Youth (2010). *Recommitting to Our Nation's Youth: Building on the Legacy of Youth Opportunity Implications for Federal Policy.*

Decision Information Resources (2007). *Youth Opportunity Grants Initiative: Impact and Synthesis Report.*

Decision Information Resources (2007). *Youth Opportunity Grants Initiative: Management Information Systems Report – Revised Final.*

Decision Information Resources (2007). *Youth Opportunity Grant Initiative: Process Evaluation Final Report.*

Dubois, David L. (2006). *Youth Mentoring: Programs and Practices that Work, Forum Brief.* Washington, DC: American Youth Policy Forum.

Ehrle Macomber, Jennifer, Mike Pergamit, Tracy Vericker, Daniel Kuehn, Marla McDaniel, Erica H. Zielewski, Adam Kent, and Heidi Johnson (2009). *Multiple Pathways Connecting to School and Work.* Washington, DC: Urban Institute.

Esterle, John, and Chris Gates (2010). *Civic Pathways Out of Poverty and Into Opportunity.* Washington, DC: Philanthropy for Active Civic Engagement.

Fernandez, Adrienne (2007). *Vulnerable Youth: Background and Policies.* Washington, DC: Congressional Research Service.

Foster-Bey, John, Nathan Dietz, and Robert Grimm, Jr. (2006). *Volunteers Mentoring Youth: Implications of Closing the Mentoring Gap.* Washington, DC: Corporation for National and Community Service.

Gan, Katherine N., JoAnn Jastrzab, Anna Jefferson, Glen Schneider, and Caroline Shlager (2011). *Youth Corps Emerging Practices for Education and Employment.* Boston, MA: Abt Associates.

Ganzglass, Evelyn Harris, and Linda Harris (2008). *Creating Postsecondary Pathways to Good Jobs for Young High School Dropouts: The Possibilities and the Challenges.* Washington, DC: Center for American Progress.

Grimm, Robert, Kevin Cramer, LaMonica Shelton, Nathan Dietz, Lillian Dote, and Shelby Jennings (2008). *Still Serving: Measuring the Eight-Year Impact of AmeriCorps on Alumni.* Washington, DC: Corporation for National and Community Service.

Grobe, Terry, Kate O'Sullivan, Sally T. Prouty, and Sarah White (2011). *A Green Career Pathways Framework: Postsecondary and Employment Success for Low-Income, Disconnected Youth.* Washington, DC: The Corps Network.

Grubb, W. Norton (2003). *Using Community Colleges to Re-Connect Disconnected Youth.* New York: Community College Research Center, Institute on Education and the Economy, Teachers College, Columbia University.

Hair, Elizabeth, Kristin Moore, Thomas Ling, Cameron McPhee-Baker, and Brett Brown (2009). *Youth Who are 'Disconnected' and Those Who Then Reconnect: Assessing the Influence of Family, Programs, Peers and Communities.* Washington, DC: Child Trends.

Hanleybrown, Fay, John Kania, and Mark Kramer. "Channeling Change: Making Collective Impact Work." *Stanford Social Innovation Review,* January 2012 ed.

Hastings, Sara, Rhonda Tsoi-A-Fatt, and Linda Harris (2010). *Building a Comprehensive Youth Employment System: Examples of Effective Practice.* Washington, DC: Center for Law and Social Policy.

Hooker, S. and Brand, B. (2009). *Success at Every Step: How 23 Programs Support Youth on the Path to College and Beyond.* Washington, DC: American Youth Policy Forum.

Kania, John, and Mark Kramer. "Collective Impact." *Stanford Social Innovation Review,* Winter 2011 ed.

KIDS COUNT. *Indicator Brief: Reducing the Number of Disconnected Youth (2009).* Baltimore, MD: The Annie E. Casey Foundation.

Maguire, Sheila, Joshua Freely, Carol Clymer, Maureen Conway, and Deena Schwartz (2010). *Tuning into Local Labor Markets: Findings from the Sectoral Employment Impact Study.* Philadelphia, PA: Private/Public Ventures.

Manyika, James, Susan Lund, Byron Auguste, Lenny Mendonca, Tim Welsh, and Sreenivas Ramaswamy (2011). *An Economy that Works: Job Creation and America's Future.* McKinsey Global Institute.

McKnaught Yonkman, Mary, and John Marshall Bridgeland (2009). *All Volunteer Force from Military to Civilian Service.* Washington, DC: Civic Enterprises.

Millenky, Megan, Dan Bloom, Sara Muller-Ravett, and Joseph Broadus (2011). *Staying on Course: Three-Year Results of the National Guard Youth ChalleNGe Evaluation.* New York: MDRC.

O'Connor, Jenn, and Tom Hilliard (2009). *Back on Track: Re-Connecting New Yorks Disconnected Youth to Education and Employment.* New York: Schuyler Center for Analysis and Advocacy.

O'Connor, Robert (2006). *Mentoring in America 2005: A Snapshot of the Current State of Mentoring.* Alexandria, VA: MENTOR.

Pathways to Prosperity Project (2011). *Pathways to Prosperity: Meeting the Challenge of Preparing Young Americans for the 21st Century.* Boston, MA: Harvard Graduate School of Education.

Ready by 21, Credentialed by 26 Series (2011). *When Working Works: Employment and Postsecondary Success.*

Riley, Michael Chavez (2009). *Building a Better Bridge: Helping Youth to Enter and Succeed in College.* New York: Youth Development Institute, a Program of the Tides Center.

Saito, Rebecca N., and Dr. Cynthia L. Sipe (2006). *The National Agenda for Action: Background and Analysis of Mentoring Today.* Alexandria, VA: MENTOR.

Shelton, LaMonica, Brooke Nicholas, Lillian Dote, and Robert Grimm (2007). *AmeriCorps: Changing Lives, Changing America – A Report on AmeriCorps' Impact on Members and Non-Profit Organizations.* Washington, DC: Corporation for National and Community Service.

Sipe, Cynthia L. (1996). *Mentoring: A Synthesis of P/PV's Research 1988-1995.* Philadelphia: Private/Public Ventures.

Steinberg, Adria and Cheryl Almeida (2011). *Pathway to Recovery: Implementing a Back on Track through College Model.* Boston, MA: Jobs for the Future.

Stuhldreher, Anne and Rourke Obrien (2011). *Family Independence Initiative: New Approach to Help Families Exit Poverty.* Washington, DC: New America Foundation.

Treschan, Lazar, and David Jason Fischer (2009). *From Basic Skills to Better Futures: Generating Economic Dividends for New York City.* New York: The Community Service Society.

U.S. Census Bureau (2004). *Educational Attainment in the United States: 2003 Population Characteristics.*

U.S. Congressional Research Service (2009). *Disconnected Youth: A Look at 16- to 24-Year Olds Who Are Not Working or In School.*

Wald, Michael, and Tia Martinez (2003). *Connected by 25: Improving the Life Chances of the Country's Most Vulnerable 14-24 Year Olds.* Prepared for William and Flora Hewlett Foundation.

Weeter, C. and Martin, N. (2011). *Building Roads to Success: Key Considerations for Communities and States Reconnecting Youth to Education.* Washington, DC: National Youth Employment Coalition.

WESTAT and METIS ASSOCIATES (2011). *CEO Young Adult Literacy Program and the Impact of Adding Paid Internships: NYC Center for Economic Opportunity Evaluation.*

White House Task Force for Disadvantaged Youth (2003). *Final Report.*

Wight, Vanessa, Michelle Chau, Yumiko Aratani, Susan Wile Schwarz, and Kalyani Thampi (2010). *A Profile of Disconnected Young Adults in 2010.* New York: National Center for Children of Poverty, Columbia University.

Youth Transition Funders Group (2010). *Connected by 25: Effective Policy Solutions for Vulnerable Youth, Issue Brief.*